ENDORSE

"This book is fantastic! At a time when people are walking away from the Church and fail to see the relevance of faith, Bishop Székely has given us a means by which we can reach these souls. Most often, they have already rejected the voice of the Shepherd, looking to science, philosophy, the arts, or some other area to provide the answers to their questions. In this book, the bishop uses these exact means to demonstrate the truth of God's revelation. This book is excellent for everyone because it teaches the same truths the Church has always taught, but from a new and fresh perspective. The perennial challenge for catechists is to present the truth in a way the audience can best receive it. In a time when faith is being lost by so many, this book provides a way to touch the hearts of those who are searching for the truth but think the Church does not have the answers. The goodness, truth, and beauty, in any discipline, leads us always to the One who is good, true, and beautiful: Jesus Christ, Our Lord."

—Fr. Robert Altier, Parochial Vicar, Holy Trinity Parish, South St. Paul, MN
Author of the book, God's Plan for Your Marriage

"The Door of Faith is a modern and compelling illumination of eternal truth. It is a great help to educators, to believers who seek to understand the Catholic faith, and to all people of good will."

—His Eminence Cardinal, Doctor Péter Erdő, Archbishop of Budapest,
Primate of Hungary

"In this illuminating book, *The Door of Faith*, Bishop and Doctor János Székely shows us that faith and reason belong together and support one another. Indeed, faith is truly like a door, a passage to the infinite for which we were made. Infinite, too, is the happiness that everyone longs for, and that can truly be found through the door of faith."

—Fr. Anthony Blount, SOLT
Vicar General of the Society of Our Lady of the Most Holy Trinity

"A great sensitivity and holy compassion flowed from Bishop János Székely, as I sat comfortably with him in his residence at the Chancery in Szombathely, a beautiful city and diocese in Western Hungary, near the Austrian border. We were praying and discussing in earnest the present and urgent state of affairs in his homeland and throughout Europe, the "Old Continent." What a wonderful gift it was to share and converse heart-to-heart with a Church leader both learned and kind, both scholarly and humble; and one who also possessed a hunger and eagerness to reach out far and wide and embrace all of humanity with his amazing discovery. He has encountered the potency and Truth of the Words and Life of the God-man, Jesus Christ, our sole and utterly capable Redeemer, and His certain promises of PURPOSE, NEW LIFE, and JOY, here and hereafter...

Bishop János, surely a man and pastor after God's own Heart, has himself walked through the holy door of faith and has caught a glimpse of nothing less than paradise, the joy of man's desire. Jesus is calling. Our brother bishop is beckoning; blest shall we be if we follow him to and through the Portal, the Resurrected and Living DOOR to PEACE, MEANING, CONTENTMENT, and everlasting FULFILLMENT. Give this gift of *The Door of Faith* to others who are searching... and to yourself. "COME, and you will SEE!"

 —*Fr. Jim Blount, SOLT*
 International Teaching, Healing, and Deliverance Ministry

"This book presents to you the gate after which there are no more gates. It is the gate you are searching for, the gate of ultimate human dignity, the gate for people rejected by the world, the gate that is pure gift. Come and see, for on this gate is written your name."

 —*Richard James, Pakistani refugee, living in Church-provided housing*
 in Szombathely, Hungary

"Apologetics is not an easy genre, especially in a world where faith is sometimes viewed as incompatible with reason. This clearly written book shows how this is not the case. It is authored by someone who is not only a well-versed theologian with a keen eye on literature and the arts, but also a pastor who knows from experience the questions and doubts that enter the searcher's mind. It is a superb introduction to the Catholic faith for both adult seekers and Catholics who wish to deepen their faith and better understanding the truths upholding their belief."

 —*Sister Hedvig Deák of the Apostolic Congregation of the Dominican*
 Sisters in Hungary and Professor of Church History

"The author's reflections on the modern state of human condition and the profound crisis of hope and faith are interspersed with the poetry of Hungarian, Italian, and French poets. This gives the whole book an aesthetic touch, a flare that warms the heart of the reader in the quest for the meaning of life sought in the depths of beauty.

The leading motif of the book recalls the homily of John Paul II during the inauguration of his pontificate on October 16, 1978: "Do not be afraid. Open, I say open wide the doors for Christ." Briefly explaining the principal truths concerning Christianity in the context of its history and its presence in the world of today, the monograph does not only adduce reliable historical, scientific, moral, and theological truths, but at the same time, it constitutes a personal witness to Jesus Christ and to His saving power, as perceived and experienced by bishop Székely himself. From this perspective, it is a personal account of opening the door to Christ from within his own heart."

—*Henryk Drawnel, Professor of Old Testament Apocrypha at the University of Lublin, Poland*

When the Almighty appeared to Moses, he presented himself as: I Am Y-H-V-H! An unusual name. If we look at it more closely, we see that the past, the present, and the future form of the Hebrew verb "to be" is forged into it. That is: "I Am the One Who was, Who is, and Who will be!"

I pray that this book by János Székely helps you to find the answers to the questions living in you, as Moses found the answers on the day when God revealed to him His wonderful Name.

- Where has God appeared in your past?
- Do you sense God in your present?
- At what point in your future do you want God to stand at Your side?

—*Zoltán Radnóti, Chief Rabbi of Hungary*

THE
DOOR
of
FAITH

Bishop and Doctor
János Székely

©2024 Queen of Peace Media
All rights reserved.
www.QueenofPeaceMedia.com
Novato, California

An E-Book Edition (2024) is also available. Books may be purchased in quantity by contacting the publisher directly at orders@queenofpeacemedia.com.

ISBN-13: 978-1-947701-24-3

CONTENTS

FOREWORD

Today there is a crisis of faith and hope in the hearts of many. People are confused and seeking distractions because they are sitting in the uncomfortable silence of life and haven't yet found the peace and joy they had hoped for. Many are wandering down roads of promise with hidden dead ends, searching chaotically for happiness and meaning in a world that has failed them. People want something more than what they have. Consciously or not, they are seeking something that will anchor them to a shore of safety, give them a hope that is eternal, and the promise of a love that will never disappoint.

There are answers to this searching and longing, this perennial knocking in every human heart. And the answers can be found in this book. Using an engaging style accessible to every curious reader, from adolescence to old age, Bishop and Doctor János Székely has masterfully accomplished the near impossible. He has explored the essence of human life on planet earth through the lenses of science, history, philosophy, morality, and religion, and he has succeeded in revealing the meaning of life and the existence of God.

Are you seeking answers to the innate questions deep within yourself, which are common to all mankind, such as, Why am I here? What is life all about? Is this all there is? Then there is no time to delay. The questions in your heart need answers, if not for yourself, then for those to whom you could transmit your knowledge, if you but had a better understanding of your faith.

The Door of Faith will not disappoint, no matter your personal starting point. It mixes in the beauty of poetry with the primacy of examined facts, speaking to the mind, while whispering to the soul. It is alive and breathing with the Spirit that animates the world, the same Spirit that animates you and me.

You are invited to connect with that Spirit. You are invited to turn the page... and open the door to faith.

—*Christine Watkins, MTS, LCSW*

Author of The Warning: Testimonies and Prophecies of the Illumination of Conscience, Winning the Battle for Your Soul, *and many other books.*

A CALL
TO ENTER THROUGH
THE DOOR

INTRODUCTION

During a trip I once made, I was talking with a famous nuclear physicist for hours. He told me that he had been raised in a completely atheistic environment somewhere in the former Czechoslovakia and admitted that he had not been baptized, nor had his wife and children. His life, a "successful" one, no doubt, was fraught with stress and hardships, as he explained. He said that on weekends, time permitting, he would escape to one of the hills near the city, climb up to its top, and sit there for one or two hours on his own. There, "I watch this enchantingly beautiful world around me," he confessed, "and I pour out my heart. I get a feeling as if someone is listening to me, and I always come home relieved." Then he added, "I guess this could be what you Christians call prayer."

How remarkable it is: a completely unbelieving person still feels, at the bottom of his heart, that there is somebody listening to him, somebody who knows him and can see him and will lend an ear to his cries.

Dear Reader,

This little book has been written for people who, like this nuclear physicist, can sometimes feel a "knocking" in the depths of their hearts: people with questions, people who see the panoramas of this world with admiration and who wonder, "Where does all this beauty come from, and what is it good for?" or "Why am I alive? Who sees my pain? What am I supposed to do? What can I hope for?"

The content of this book is provided by someone for whom faith in God has always been a given. I began serving around the altar at the age of five. I could not understand anything from all that was said in the church, but I was instantly captured and mesmerized by the atmosphere of the services and the aura of the house of God. I am extremely grateful to my parents for leading me there, as well as for their authentic lives, which enabled me to easily follow the path travelled by them. When I was fourteen, I read the entire Old Testament from cover to cover within a few weeks during a summer vacation.

That was a tremendous experience. As I sat by Lake Balaton, I gazed at the poplars on the shore and the clouds in the sky, and I felt again and again that the words of the Bible came from out there. Even though I did not understand many of the events, images, and customs in Biblical history, I was aware of and infused with the enormous power and beauty of the Scriptures.

To put it differently, this book was written by an individual who, by God's grace, has always been a believer. At the same time, I am someone who keeps asking questions, who has often sat at the bedside of the dying, seen the misery of the African continent, and heard the cries of the afflicted.

I decided to write because I can see many people are held back on the road to faith by questions and objections of reason and theory. In my view, our contemporary western culture is dying as a direct consequence of severing ties with the Creator and the Spring of Life.

I have endeavored to offer brief and succinct answers to the most fundamental questions.

I start out with the assumption that busy people of today generally do not appreciate lengthy explanations.

A painter, Holman Hunt, created a picture of Christ standing at the door and knocking. The peculiarity of the painting is that the door has no handle and can only be opened from the inside. The Book of Revelation uses the following expression: "Behold, I stand at the door and knock. If anyone hears my voice and opens the door, I will enter his house and dine with him, and he with me" (Rev. 3:20).

Dear Reader,
  Your Creator is knocking gently on the door of your life, as well. Wherever Christ is welcomed, He will bring blessings and life to that place.

This sound of gentle knocking is described by the Hungarian poet Endre Ady (1877-1919) in this way:

I Should Love to Be Loved
by Endre Ady

I am neither infant nor sir
Nor parent, nor lover
Of anyone, of anyone.
I am, as every man is, Majesty,
The North Point, the Mystery, the Stranger,
A fleeting wisp of light.
A fleeting wisp of light.
But alas! I cannot remain this way.
I should like to show myself to the world,
So that someone sees me, so that someone sees me.
This is why I sing and I torment myself.
I should love to be loved.
I wish to be someone's, I wish to be someone's.

I. The Unavoidable Question

"...all the labors of the ages, all the devotion, all the inspiration, all the noonday brightness of human genius, are destined to extinction in the vast death of the solar system, and the whole temple of man's achievement must inevitably be buried beneath the debris of a universe in ruins – all these things, if not quite beyond

dispute, are yet so nearly certain, that no philosophy which rejects them can hope to stand. Only within the scaffolding of these truths, only on the firm foundation of unyielding despair, can the soul's habitation henceforth be safely built."

—Russell, Bertrand, "A Free Man's Worship," *Why I Am Not a Christian*, (ed. P. Edwards; New York City, 1957) p. 107.

"There's probably no God. Now stop worrying and enjoy your life."

(sign on buses in England)

Many people think that the ultimate questions of life cannot be answered. Is there a reason for the existence of the world? Does it have a purpose? Does anything happen after we die? Are there any universally valid moral principles? They believe these questions are of such magnitude as to exceed the limits of human understanding. According to many, inquiries like these need not even concern us. They argue that our only objective should be to ensure that the short time that we are given to live may preferably be spent in a pleasant way.

But why is it important to ask these ultimate fundamental questions?

1. What are you doing?

A traveler was approaching a city under construction. His journey took him across an enormous quarry. He saw that the laborers were working with drops of sweat on their bodies and grit covering their bitter-looking faces. He went up to one of them and asked him, "What are you doing?", to which the person replied, "Can't you see? I'm breaking stones." The traveler went up to another worker and asked him the same question, "What are you doing?" The man retorted angrily, "I am making money to support my family!" The traveler went on and finally caught sight of someone who was apparently working with a great deal of satisfaction and joy. He asked this man, too, "What are you doing?" The person straightened his back and answered with a shining face, "I am building a cathedral."

They were all doing the same job, breaking stones and making money, yet in slightly different ways. We all live the same life: we are born, we study, we grow, we work, we fall ill, and we die. But there are people who travel this journey differently—with glittering eyes. These people do not merely break stones and make money... They know that they are part of the construction of a great cathedral. They are aware that this world was created out of love, that it is moved by love, and it will be brought to fulfillment by love.

This is how the Hungarian poet Dezső Kosztolányi, who was once an atheist, put it, expressing his sorrow when he discovered this secret only in old age:

Daybreak Drunkenness
by Dezső Kosztolá

I would tell you this—I hope it won't bore you.
Last night I stopped working at three
and went to bed.
But the machine in my mind was rattling on,
and though I tried to sleep, all I managed
was tossing and turning furiously instead.
Yet I went on, poisoned lullabies invoking,
calling out for sleep to come, imploring—
no use.
So I got up, ignoring it all,
pacing up and down in a nightshirt
in my room—stumbling like a drunk
to the front window, I happened to look out.

Wait, how should I begin, how can I explain?
You know my home, the site,
and if you recall my bedroom, you will remember
how deserted the street is there
at that time of the night.
Through the window you can peer into open flats.
Broken and blind
the people horizontally lie

in their beds with eyes turned up into
the mist of their minds
since the cancer of everyday existence
covers them up like blankets.
Even the house is asleep, dead and dumb,
just as it will be after a hundred numb
years, when as ruins it will lie
with grass appearing in the cracks,
and no one will know whether it was a home
or a pigsty.

But up there, my friend, up there is the radiant sky.
And the stars
whose breathing souls shine in the silence
of the lukewarm autumn night
which precedes the cold—
it was they, the stars,
who yonder and from afar
gazed at Hannibal's army
and now are gazing at me.
I don't know what happened to me at that moment,
but it seemed a pair of wings fluttered above me,
and something I had long buried,
my childhood, was bending down towards me.

For so long
was I gazing at the marvels of the sky
that it turned red on the eastern horizon,
and the wind made the stars swing in the firmament,
and an immense shaft of light
flared in the distance.
The gates of a heavenly hall flung open,
torches were lighted all around,
something flickered.
The guests were dispersing,
in the deep half-lit shadows of the dawn.
The portico still swam in brightness,
and standing on the steps,
a grand lord, a king of heaven and court
was bidding farewell.
Movement, the impatient jingling of ringing bells,
and quiet whispers of ladies were heard,
as when the ball is over
and the doormen shout for carriage and coach.

A lace veil was seen to descend
from the distance,
like a net of diamonds
onto a brilliant blue cloak
that a dear and beautiful woman had donned.
And upon her a diadem
was shining with the light of pure peace.
And silently, like a dream,
she glided into a swaying carriage,
and with a smile, drove away
amidst the sparkling hooves of hundreds of horses
and showers of silvery confetti
on the torchlit Milky Way.

Gaping, I stood
and shouted with happiness:
There is a ball in the sky, a ball every night!
Until sunrise
I stood motionless gazing.
Then I said to myself:
What were you seeking
on this earth, what old wives' tales
what harlots were keeping you captive,
for what scribblings were you so active,
that so many summers and winters passed by
and so many a slovenly night
without noticing the ball in the sky?

Fifty,
oh fifty years, my heart recoils,
my deaths here and there are more and more.
And yet for fifty years, still sparkling above me as before
are all these bright living neighbors in the heavens
who can see my tears as I shed them.
Well, I tell you the truth,
I fell to my knees and thanked them.

To the blue heavens I started to sing,
to him whom I search for in vain, while alive or when dead later—
whom no one knows where to find, here or in the ether.
But now as my muscles relax, just
so, I have a feeling, my friend, that in the dust,
where I was stumbling among briers and souls,
I was the guest of a grand and unknown Lord.[1]

[1] Translation by Tamás Kabdebó, *Hundred Hungarian Poems*, (Albion Editions, Manchester:

What a shame it is for someone to struggle and travel through his or her existence without coming to appreciate the true depths and perspectives of life. Therefore, it is important to ask the great and ultimate questions. Those who fail to do so lose much.

Saint Augustine of Hippo was someone who virtually ran from God, the Mysterious Hunter. Although he felt God's steps behind him, he was fleeing from Him. When at last he opened the doors of his life before Him, he wrote painfully:

"Late have I loved you, beauty so old and so new: late have I loved you. And see, you were within, and I was in the external world and sought you there, and in my unlovely state, I rushed heedlessly into those lovely, created things which you made. You were with me, but I was not with you ... You called and cried out loud and shattered my deafness. You were radiant and resplendent, you put to flight my blindness..."

— St. Augustine of Hippo, Confessions

1976). Adapted and copy-edited by Christine Watkins.

Many people who have come to faith say, in retrospect, that while they were living without faith, their lives were bleak, empty and dull. Nothing could fill their hearts completely. Research has repeatedly demonstrated that faith also has a positive effect on physical health—a general sense of wellbeing and life expectancy. People of faith live longer, are more satisfied and enjoy a better physical condition than their nonbelieving peers.[2]

2. Agnosticism in practice is impossible

Many believe that since we cannot answer the great questions of life, it is better to maintain a sense of uncertainty in this respect. It cannot be known for sure if God exists, whether there is a reason and purpose for the existence of the world, and if death is followed by anything. It may well seem as though agnosticism was the humble attitude of an

educated person because, after all, the ultimate questions are beyond the abilities of humans.

Interestingly though, agnosticism is not viable in practice. At every moment of our lives, we human beings must always make decisions: whether to live and start a new day, believe that life is meaningful, that there are unconditional moral norms, that there is something after death—or, rather, that humans are an evolutionary error, that

---

[2] Cf. Koening, Harold George and Lawson, Douglas M., Faith in the Future: Healthcare, Aging and the Role of Religion (Conshohocken, 2004), pp. 78-79; Kopp, Mária and Kovács, Mónika Erika, A magyar népesség életminősége az ezredfordulón [Quality of life in Hungary at the dawn of the new millennium] (Budapest, 2006), p. 8.

there are no unconditional moral laws, and that there is nothing after death. In practice, we make a choice—a declared or implicit one—between these two basic options every minute of every day.[3]

Whether people are able to tolerate illness or loss, able to forgive a severe insult, able to sacrifice themselves for someone else, or able to be wholeheartedly happy, all depends upon how they see and live their lives—whether they are building a cathedral or simply breaking stones and making money.

There is a passage in the Gospel where Jesus is asked where His authority comes from. In return, Jesus asks them where the baptism of John[4] came from: God or man? Senior members of the clergy do not give an answer because they know that if they said it was from God, Jesus would ask why they did not believe Him, as His authority also came from heaven; conversely, if they said the authority of John's baptizing was from man, they would need to be afraid of the people since John was considered a prophet by all. They answered, "We don't know." Jesus is infuriated by the absence of an answer to the question and refuses to reply to the question directed at Him (cf. Mark 11:27-33).

These priests do not want to answer Jesus's critical question: could God speak, and did He, in fact, speak through John? Their courage fails them; they do not even bother to say no. This is the most radical type of denial: they do not even deign to answer the question.

Agnosticism is often like this:

"Does God exist or doesn't He?"

"I don't know; I don't care; I won't give an answer. I don't think there is an answer."

When a spouse declines to answer their wife's or husband's question, it may amount to rejection of the rudest kind, suggesting, "I don't care about you. For me, you don't exist."

Agnosticism is often nothing but a radical "no" to God.

Of course, there are people who feel that they do not know the ultimate answers, but they try to travel the journey of their lives on the path of honesty and decency, remaining open to a possible answer and continuously looking for it. This book happens to be aimed at such searching individuals.

3. The fundamental questions of life are also important from the point of view of the existence of humanity

If the following question remains shrouded in mystery—whether there is meaning and purpose for the existence of the world, or to put it differently, whether the world reflects design and orderliness—then it will

---

[3] Ratzinger, Joseph (Pope Benedict XVI), "Europe in the Crisis of Cultures." Communio 32 (Summer, 2005), pp. 345-346; cf. Mesiru, Vittori, Ipotesi su Gesú (Torino, 1977) p. 22.
[4] John the Baptist

also continue to be a mystery whether there are moral obligations that apply to everyone. In that case, it becomes uncertain whether a human being is only a representative of a particular species, a smart animal who may eventually be sacrificed on the altar of progress, or whether a human being is created by God and represents infinite value to the Creator, and therefore the life of every single individual—including an unborn baby in its mother's womb, a person with disabilities, and a helpless patient—is sacred and inviolable.

It is no coincidence that, despite seemingly proclaiming humanistic ideas (promoting the prosperity of the nation and creating equality), the two major autocratic systems of the 20th century—Nazism and Communism—resulted in the most horrible acts of inhumanity because both ideologies were inherently atheistic. When the Creator disappears, human dignity will also vanish. Under such circumstances, humans are degraded to smart animals that may become expendable to achieve particular goals.

In the last two hundred years, efforts have been underway to protect human dignity with legal tools (e.g., the Universal Declaration of Human Rights). However, the limited success of such attempts is well documented in history. The ultimate and only true guarantee of human dignity is God.

It is not a matter of chance that the Ten Commandments came from personal contact with God. No other laws of comparable clarity and lucidity were ever created in antiquity. Someone reading the Babylonian Law Code Stele of Hammurabi will find no mention of the duty to protect life unconditionally. If, for instance, the son of a guarantor died as a result of harsh treatment, the son of the lender (and murderer) was to be killed. If the slave of the guarantor died because of the maltreatment applied (as a measure in the process of debt collection) the lender (and murderer) had to pay ⅓ of a mina of silver in compensation.[5]

According to the teachings of the religion of ancient Egypt, pharaohs were the children of the gods. The name Ramses means "son of the god Ra"; Thutmose means "son of the god Thoth". The pharaoh was believed to be protected by the god. Questions as to whether the tears of the poor, miserable slaves would reach this god were not really addressed by the religions of the ancient East.[6]

In antiquity, the life of a slave was often not even worth as much as that of an animal. The Emperor Caligula (AD 37-41), for instance,

---

[5] CH § 115-116. Clarity and explicitness on issues of morality are also missing in Assyrian laws. For example, these laws prescribed a death sentence for a woman who robbed her husband (LMA § 3). If a virgin was seduced, the seducer, among other things, had to surrender his own wife to the father of the girl (LMA § 55).
[6] Cf. Pritchard, James, *Ancient Near Eastern Texts Relating to the Old Testament* (Princeton, 1969): "I will praise the Lord of wisdom II, pp. 1-5. 33-37; "I implored the god, but he did not turn his countenance; I prayed to my goddess, but she did not raise her head..." pp. 434-435.

ordered that his animal entourage marshaled for the circus games be fed with the flesh of slaughtered slaves. However, the true living God, to whom even the lowest slave is infinitely precious, appeared in history and revealed Himself to Moses. This is how God told Moses to transmit His words to the Pharaoh: "So you shall say to Pharaoh: Thus says the LORD: Israel is my son, my first-born. Hence I tell you: Let my son go..." (Ex. 4:22-23). The life of even the lowest slave is infinitely valuable to God. This realization gives rise to the Ten Commandments. Everyone's life, even of the lowest slave, the unborn baby, and the helpless elderly person, is sacred. Therefore, you shall not kill! Everyone's spouse is sacred and inviolable. Therefore, you shall not commit adultery! Everyone's property is inviolable. Therefore, you shall not steal!

If humankind comes to the conclusion that there is no reason and purpose for the existence of the world, and it lacks an objective order, then morality (i.e., harmony with this objective order) will disappear and so will the possibility for objective truth. At that point, who is to say when it is wrong to punish someone who felt justified in killing somebody? Why is it wrong, then, if a billionaire condemns poor countries to destitution? Is it only because the majority see this to be the case and vote on legislation to this effect? And what if they change their minds tomorrow?

4. The question inexorably arises

This world was not created by us, and we were not the ones who laid down its laws. It is as if we have suddenly found ourselves sitting on a train that is moving at full speed in a specific direction. After a while, it seems logical that each of us would begin to ask ourselves from where and to where this train is heading. It wouldn't seem particularly sensible to inquire only about the location of the dining car.

The question of whether there is a reason and purpose for our existence arises in every human being with a loving heart—if not before, then when they sit at the deathbeds of their loved ones. As the question cannot be sidestepped, it may well be worth our considering it earlier, as well.

5. You are a human, so you ask questions

No one asked us whether we wanted to live as human beings. We have been thrown into the deep end of the great adventure of existence. A person is a kind of being that is not satisfied by this visible and tangible world. We possess a certain type of hunger that no earthly bread may satiate. Consequently, human beings ask questions about the cause and purpose of the visible and tangible world in order to find out if there is something beyond this finite earthly existence.

You are a human, so you ask questions. Do not shy away from the hard but rewarding challenge of finding the answers.[7]

---

[7] Saint Augustine of Hippo says that doubting is an essential human characteristic. However, there is one thing that cannot be doubted: Whoever doubts exists and trusts in some sort of truth (*De Trinitate* 10,10.14-16).

6. Can life worthy of a human being be built on nothing?

This chapter began with a quote from Bertrand Russell on radical pessimism, which—as he argues—ought to be the foundation upon which any human work is built. In my understanding, no life worthy of a human being may be based on this kind of pessimism. Such a foundation would have been insufficient for the self-sacrifice of Father Maximilian Kolbe and inadequate to inspire Mozart's Requiem or Michelangelo's Pietà, and it would fail to engender sincere forgiveness, genuine joy, and a true sense of peace.

Of course, there are some people identifying themselves as non-believers who live their lives and act in strikingly unselfish ways. However, these acts of theirs testify to their very belief in something greater than them and even powerful enough to make them renounce themselves. They prove this faith of theirs with their deeds. Conversely and regrettably, there are people claiming to be believers who are appallingly self-centered and cannot see past their own drives, complaints, and fixations, thereby often becoming unbearable to those around them. Through their actions, they prove that, apart from themselves, they do not believe in anything, and nothing could make them renounce themselves. It is their deeds that provide evidence of their lack of faith.

In proposing that, without faith, the life of humankind will become inhuman, I think not only of faith expressed through words, but genuine faith, which raises us above ourselves and our selfishness.

Let us then set about tackling the questions and finding some possible answers!

The famous writer, Anne Lamott, was raised in a hippie family in California. In her childhood, no limitations were imposed on her. After finishing her studies, she returned to California and started to live the life of a hippie herself. She would consume cocaine and alcohol in vast amounts. Engaging in sexual relationships with many men, she became pregnant and had an abortion.

She ended up in extreme distress. In such a state of mind, she would sometimes stop by a Presbyterian church. She would enjoy listening to the choir singing and feel some sense of peace. She would always leave the church before the sermon.

One night, after drinking rather heavily, she suddenly had a strong sensation of the presence of someone in her room. She knew that it was none other than Christ. She was by no means ready to receive Him. Faced with the prospect of abandoning her old hippie lifestyle and her "buddies," she exclaimed aloud, "No way. I'd rather die!"

However, this was not the end of the story. She could no longer rid herself of the feeling that, in her bedraggled life, Christ was there in her most bitter moments, willing to help her, and from time to time, drawing near like a kitten, as Lamott put it. She felt that once she let

Him in, once she opened the door and gave Him milk, He would stay there for good.

A week later, she entered the church again and sat down in a pew. She was in such bad shape that she was unable to move, so she remained seated until the service was over. The last song moved her deeply. She ran home, but all along the way felt that the "cat" was following her from behind. The breathtakingly blue sky was shining bright. When she opened her front door, she lowered her head and said, "I'll give up. All right. You can come in." This was the pivotal moment of her conversion.[8]

A Jewish atheist doctor named Boris Nikolayevich Kornfeld was sent to one of the gulags of the Soviet Union. He noticed that an elderly Russian prisoner was always serene and calm, even in that hell on earth. Curious to find out what could be the secret behind this strange phenomenon, he sat down next to the old man in order to listen to him. The old man was a believer, and this was the source of his serenity. He would speak extensively to Kornfeld about Jesus's words and deeds. He even taught him the Lord's Prayer. Kornfeld was especially touched by this sentence: "Forgive us our trespasses, as we forgive those who trespass against us." Kornfeld considered this line to be remarkable. Then a few weeks later, the old man died.

Soon afterwards, a knifing incident happened among the soldiers guarding the prisoners. One of the soldiers suffered a severe injury and was brought to Kornfeld in the small hospital barracks of the camp in order to save his life. Kornfeld recognized the soldier as one of the most ruthless guards. The thought that he could bandage the wound in a way that the soldier would bleed to death crossed his mind. "He would deserve that," he said to himself silently. But he was suddenly terrified by this prospect. As a doctor, he had reached a point where he could cause the death of a human being. And then he uttered the words from the Lord's Prayer: "Forgive us our trespasses, as we forgive those who trespass against us." He operated on the soldier and dressed his wound so that he would survive. In Kornfeld's heart, faith sprung forth. From time to time, he would even talk about Jesus to the patients in the hospital barracks as he recalled the stories told by the old man.

One evening, a Russian prisoner in critical condition was brought to the barracks. The alarming expression on his face spoke of despair and utter hopelessness. Kornfeld took a seat by his bed and talked to him about Jesus for hours. He also said the Lord's Prayer several times. However, the guards had noticed that Kornfeld had begun minding the prisoners' souls, as well as their bodies, and they did not approve of that. That night, as he rose from this patient's bed to go to sleep, they hit Kornfeld's head from behind with an iron cudgel. He died

---

[8] Bausch, William J., *Once Upon a Gospel: Inspiring Homilies and Insightful Reflections* (New London: 2007), pp. 51-53.

immediately. The light of faith, however, was hardly extinguished in that prison camp. The patient Kornfeld had talked to for hours on the last night of his life was slowly recuperating, and a fervent faith was developing in his heart. The man was Alexander Solzhenitsyn, a future writer of world renown, who in 1970 was awarded the Nobel Prize in Literature.

II. The Starry Sky above Me

"Two things fill the mind with ever new and increasing admiration and reverence...: the starry sky above me and the moral law within me."

Kant, Immanuel, (*The Critique of Practical Reason* Hackett Publishing Company, Inc., Indianapolis/Cambridge, 2002), p. 203.

Presence
by György Rónay

Look up to the sky: there is a presence
between the clouds and the stars.

Look about you on earth:
there is a presence in grass, in flowers,
in the amazed eyes of animals,
on people's faces.

Dig beneath the ground:
the footprints of intention
are looming towards you
from bones and from fossils.

Unseen everywhere. Seen in everything.

The first step on the road to faith in God is amazement—
amazement at this enchantingly beautiful world.

1. There is a reason for things

A thinking person searches for a reason behind every phenomenon. When we hear a sound, we tend to ask where it came from or what produced it. If somebody says that he or she does not care, or even claims that it came about for no apparent reason, that person is not thinking. A wise person knows that things happen for a reason.

After a while, such a person goes on to ask where everything has come from and why it is all so marvelous and orderly. Once again, if somebody says that he or she does not care, or claims that there is no apparent reason, that person is not thinking. Something cannot evolve out of nothing by itself, and life does not issue from the inanimate automatically. Every one of the qualitative thresholds of existence seen in the world must have a sufficient reason for occurring.

When we see an enormous railway station with trains coming and going without colliding into one another, it is natural to develop the impression that there must be a schedule that someone devised, regulating how the switches are operated and the trains are routed. In fact, the way a single living cell works is far more admirable than the largest railway station; considerably more fine-tuned events take place inside the former than at the most gigantic railway station. When somebody sees this phenomenon, they will have the impression that there must be some infinite wisdom and beauty concealed behind the scenes.

2. The beginning

Perhaps to the surprise of many, modern cosmology arrived at the conclusion that there was a beginning to the material world.

Edwin Hubble, as well as other astronomers following in his footsteps, realized that the light coming to us from celestial bodies showed different bands of colors or spectra. This phenomenon came to be known as redshift.[9] It is caused by the wave properties of light: from the spectrum of the light, it is possible to make inferences about the rate of increase in the distance between the celestial body emitting that light and the Earth. Calculations of the velocities of celestial bodies led to the astonishing discovery that the material of the universe, along with space and time, had a zero point and spread out from a single spot (singularity). The age for this zero point was also established [approx. 13.7 billion years, (i.e., > 12.5 ~ < 20 billion years) ago].

In 1965, Arno Penzias and Robert Wilson demonstrated that the impact of the diffusion of the initial energy, i.e., primordial light (the so-called Big Bang), may be detected in the entire universe. This effect is known as background radiation. The current average temperature of the universe is 2.7 K.[10] In the reactions during the first few minutes of expansion following the Big Bang, as much as 23 percent of the hydrogen was converted into helium. Even the oldest objects of the universe contain 23-24 percent of helium. This fact also provides support for the Big Bang theory.[11]

Individual energy types may evolve into one another, but heat (the most irregular type of energy) cannot fully be turned back into other ("more regular") types of energy—there will always be some amount of heat energy left. If the material world was perpetual, all energy would long ago have been transformed into heat energy, and under the Law of Entropy, would have reached the state of heat death.[12] In other words, it is impossible to conceive of the universe as cyclically expanding and subsequently collapsing repeatedly. Every such collapse would increase entropy. What is more, far from slowing down, the expansion of the universe seems to be accelerating even now.

The bulk of the solid matter of the world is still hydrogen. Astronomically speaking, the world is extremely young.[13] The lifespan of atoms is finite (approx. 10^{35} years). In an exceedingly long time, our

---

[9] The phenomenon of decrease and increase in the frequency of waves (e.g., changes in the sound of a motorcycle passing by) was first described by Doppler, after whom it was named "The Doppler Effect."

[10] In other words, this means that there are approximately 300 photons within every cubic centimeter. The existence of background radiation was confirmed, and its properties were extensively described, thanks to a series of ever more precise measurements performed by NASA in 1992, and subsequently, by the European Space Agency (ESA) in 2013.

[11] Rees, Martin, *Just Six Numbers: The Deep Forces That Shape the Universe*, (Basic Books, 2000) pp. 69, 127.

[12] De la Saudée, Jacque de Bivort, *Dio, l'Uomo, l'Universo*, (Torino, 1952), pp. 96-98.

[13] Tresmontant, Claude, *L'esistenza di Dio oggi* (Modena, 1970) p. 34.

current universe, together with its stars, will eventually erode.[14]

Lately, several astronomers (Arvind Borde, Alan Guth, and Alexander Vilenkin) have demonstrated that an expanding universe endowed with five such characteristics as those of our cosmos cannot have been perpetual in the past, but must, of necessity, have had a beginning (the BGV theorem).[15] To put it differently, science has made the surprising discovery that at the zero point of space and time (i.e., the beginning), an immense amount of energy and spacetime itself appeared suddenly, and spacetime, as well as the light filling it, began to spread out. Thus, spacetime and light (i.e., energy matter) came into being. The explosion was not like that of a hand grenade but happened according to perfect mathematical harmonies and laws. It is only reasonable to ask where this energy emanation of such an unfathomable force could come from. How could it be governed—from the very first moment of its appearance—by perfect laws and harmonies?[16]

If nothing had existed in eternity (prior to the beginning of the universe), there would be nothing at the moment, either, as nothing

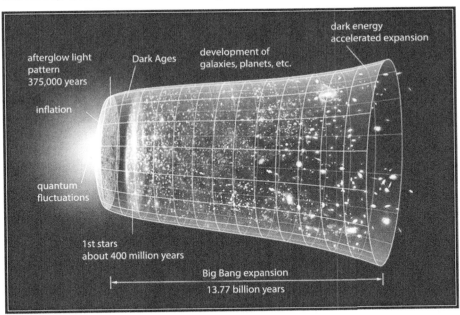

[14] Rees, p. 86.
[15] Borde, Arvin; Vilenkin, Alexander; and Guth, Alan H., "Inflationary Spacetimes Are Incomplete in Past Directions," *Physical Review Letters* 90 (2003); Vilenkin, *Many Worlds In One: The Search for Other Universes* (Hill and Wang, 2006), pp. 172-175.
[16] Cf. Guitton, Jean; Bogdanov, Igor, Bogdanov, Grichka, *Dieu et la science* (Grasset, Paris, 1991) pp. 30-31.

may only give rise to nothing.[17]

Some scientists try hard to escape the final conclusions such findings would entail. Graham Oppy, for instance, proposes an uncaused universe instead of looking for any reason.[18] Stephen Hawking, along with Andrei Linde and Leonard Susskind, suggest imagining an infinite, vibrating field or multiple universes detached from one another, in one of which, as part of the interplay of accidents, life has appeared.[19] Positing the existence of universes unrelated to us is, of course, not based on any empirical observation, but mere speculation. One needs to accept it on faith because one does not have, and cannot have, any data on it. In addition, as part of this hypothesis, the question of the beginning and cause of multiple universes also ought to be answered, and an explanation must be found as to what caused these to be aligned in a way that there would be no connection between them. The presumption of causelessness, in fact, makes it even more recognizable that the discussion is not focused on scientific findings and more on the scientist's agonizing experiments through which he or she tries to evade the final conclusions.

---

[17] Van Steenberghen, Ferdinand, *Come sappiamo che Dio esiste?* (Roma: 1966). "Nothing will come out of nothing unless the Creator, the Source of existence, exists and brings something into existence."

[18] Craig, William Lane, Reasonable Faith with William Lane Craig, "Graham Oppy on the *Kalam* Cosmological Argument," https://www.reasonablefaith.org/writings/scholarly-writings/the-existence-of-god/graham-oppy-on-the-kalam-cosmological-argument, accessed June 3, 2023.

[19] Cf. Gordon, Bruce; Dembski, William, *The Nature of Nature: Examining the Role of Naturalism in Science*, (Wilmington, 2011).

3. The miracle of life

Even though, thanks to science, we are fully familiar with every component of a simple living cell, we cannot produce one. We are unable to create an animate entity out of something inanimate. Although we may be able to slice DNA and turn animate entities into other animate entities, we cannot turn the inanimate into the animate,[20] and by no means is this an accident. The appearance of life required (and still requires) the power of the Creator, Who, like a magnet, hovers over the world, feeds information into it, and enables matter to develop and the inanimate to spawn life.[21]

An important fundamental law of inanimate matter is entropy: the increase of disorder. Energy levels are equalized: when a hot and a cold brick are placed next to each other, both will gradually become lukewarm. Life, however, works precisely against entropy. An oak tree is a huge anti-entropy- (or, to use a phrase from information theory,

---

[20] In 2010, Craig Venter made the headlines by claiming to have created life, similarly to God. However, what he did, in fact, was not create life out of the inanimate but replicate a DNA with the help of an existing one and implant it in a bacterium.

[21] Our Earth is approximately 4.5 billion years old. Life first appeared on Earth at least 3.9 billion years ago. Nowadays, it is generally understood that life existed only in a very simple form for almost 3 billion years. The first multicellular organisms emerged around 600 million years ago. The foremother of modern humankind lived in Africa approximately 170 thousand years ago.

negentropy-) factory collecting and storing up the energy of the sun, minerals, and water. It defies one of the most basic properties of inanimate substances,[22] and it does so by means of its own internal motion. Life cannot be explained from the inanimate: between the two, there is a qualitative leap, which must have a sufficient reason for happening.

4. Qualitative thresholds of existence

In the course of evolution, qualitative thresholds of existence appeared in the world. Life appeared, followed by sensation, and finally, by human reasoning and the ability to make free will decisions. These qualitative thresholds cannot be derived from lower levels of existence. Reduction fails to account for their development.[23]

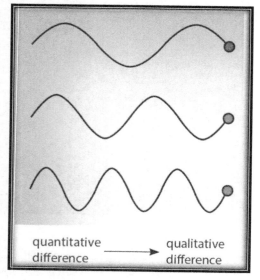

quantitative difference ⟶ qualitative difference

The perception of color by the human and the animal eye could well illustrate the point. In the world, colors do not exist in isolation from the ability of sight, but there are only beams of light of different frequencies with quantitative differences between them: some with higher and some with lower frequencies.

Humans and animals, however, do not perceive these quantitative differences—more intensive and less intensive light, but see, rather, qualitative differences of red, green and blue. Science describes how this perception develops: a beam of light enters the eye through its

---

[22] The law of increase of entropy (randomness) applies to closed systems. Here, however, the point is not about the law of entropy but the tendency of inanimate substances to move in the direction of increasing entropy. The basic tendency of life is contrary to this. Thus, life is called negentropy. Cf. Schrödinger, Erwin, *What is Life?* (Cambridge, 1944). In the famous words of the cellular biologist and Nobel Prize winner, Albert Claude, "Life is anti-entropy."

[23] A great many scientists (e.g., F. Alverdes, L. Von Bertalanffy, A. Bizzarri, H. Driesch, B. Dürken, J. S. Haldane, W. Roux, J. C. Smuts, J. V. Uexküll, G. F. Wolff, etc.) are of the view that life and cognition cannot be derived from the laws of physics and chemistry. Science, by nature, cannot even offer a justification in this regard.

"Science produces descriptions instead of proof, and its descriptions are continually open to modifications ... Science is always imprecise, only partly true and incessantly fraught with terrible simplifications." Consolmagno, Brother Guy, "The Faith of a Scientist"; from a public lecture given in Rome on 12.30.2012.

Cf. Fr. Stanley L. Jaki's booklet, *Science and Religion: A Primer* (Real View Books, 2004), p. 29.

crystalline lens, reaches the rods and cones, and the impulse travels via the optic nerve to the field of view. By providing such an account, science only answers the question of "how" but fails to address the question of "why." What "sensing red" means cannot really be defined in scientific terms, as it is not identical with light of a certain frequency, and instead speaks to the appearance of a qualitative threshold. The qualitatively more may never be derived from the qualitatively less.[24]

Reduction is not an explanation. With sensation, a qualitative plus appeared in the world. Human liberty and thought are not merely chance products of physical and chemical laws. They are not like the rustle of the reeds in the wind, reminiscent of a whisper, only vaguely imitative of real speech.

5. Accidents

As a corollary of the above, reference to mistakes does not provide an explanation for what is seen in the world[25]—not only because the number of chance accidents necessary for the evolution of life would be outright inconceivable,[26] but rather because these changes yielded qualitatively superior forms of existence. The material world is being pulled or lifted upward by something, enabling it to develop qualitatively.

Jacques Monod proposes that nature's harmony is the result of the chance interaction of false notes and mishaps. In his commentary, he admits that this is a rather absurd idea. Still, as he points out, he feels

---

[24] The Engelsian claim that quantitative changes are transformed into qualitative ones is untenable.

[25] Nobel Prize winner, Alfred Kastler, remarks that should an automated aluminum smelter with shovels collecting minerals at one end and aluminum blocks churned out at the other end be discovered on the moon, no one would think that this contrivance came into being by itself, but everyone would assume that it was created by intelligent beings. Cf. V. Marcozzi, *Caso e finatitá* (Milano: 1976), pp. 30-31. A single living cell contains 53 billion proteins, 166 billion lipid molecules, 2900 billion small molecules, 250,000 billion water and nucleic acid molecules, arrayed in an extremely delicate structure. It is a more complex and more magnificent machine than an aluminum smelter.

Practically no living creature can survive without chlorophyll or hemoglobin. In synthesizing these, the uroporphyrinogen-decarboxylase enzyme plays a pivotal role. Aided by the enzyme (produced by living cells), synthesis is complete within milliseconds. In the absence of this enzyme, however, it would take 2.3 billion years. Naturally, this is not to say that it would take 2.3 billion years for an actual hemoglobin molecule to be formed since, within that time span, the components would all decompose, too.

[26] The simplest gene of the DNA consists of 300 positions, each of which may be filled by 4 nucleotides. The probability of the formation of a biologically viable molecule as opposed to the billions of chemically possible, but biologically wrong, combinations is $1:72 \times 10^{108}$ Were the universe, with a diameter of 12.5 - 20 billion light years, to be filled with hydrogen without a vacuum, the number of atoms used for that purpose would be a 72nd of the figure cited above. Cf. Blondet, M., "Darwin addio, la vita non nacque dal Caso," *Il Giornale*, October 31, 1987; Eigen, Manfred; Winkler, Ruthild, *Il gioco: Le leggi naturali governano il Caso* (Milano: 1986).

compelled by the scientific method to avoid asking questions to which the answer has to be "God."[27]

Since science is concerned with finite material entities, it is indeed unable to measure or experimentally pinpoint God, for He is on a different level of existence. Nonetheless, it can infer Him from the impact of His actions, the existence of the universe, the marvelous order of the cosmos, and the qualitative leaps of existence found in the world. All the amazing orderliness seen in the world must have a sufficient reason.

6. The anthropological principle

Robert H. Dicke, along with other scientists, has noted that, if just a few of the basic constants of the universe were but 2 or 3 percent different, it would have been impossible for life to have appeared in the world.

Were the expansion rate of the cosmos lower in relation to gravity, the universe would soon implode. If the rate of expansion relative to gravity were higher, no galaxies, stars, or planets would have formed.

If the gravitational constant[28] were too small, there would be no supernovae or stars, in which heavier elements could form. Conversely, if it were too great, only very small and short-lived stars would have formed.

If the strong nuclear force were greater, heavy nuclei would have formed early on, and there would be no light ones left, such as hydrogen and helium, fueling stars and constituting the foundations of life. Were the strong nuclear force less intensive, no elements heavier than hydrogen could have formed.

If the weak nuclear force were greater, there would be no hydrogen because it would have been transformed into helium. The probability of the formation of the carbon atom would be very small without an excited energy level within a very narrow range. And the list could go on.[29]

---

[27] Cf. Ratzinger, Joseph, *Creazione e peccato* (Cinisello Balsamo, 1987) p. 24.
[28] Defined as the strength of gravity, which has remained unchanged for the last nine billion years. See Swinburne University of Technology. "Exploding stars prove Newton's law of gravity unchanged over cosmic time," Science Daily, March 24, 2014
https://www.sciencedaily.com/releases/2014/03/140324230254.htm, accessed July 3, 2023.
[29] The likelihood that these constants are favorable to life by chance is virtually zero. During a game of cards, a player drawing four aces 20 times in succession would be considered a matter of accident by very few. Thus, it is reasonable to ask why some people deem the appearance of the miracle of life to be the product of chance. Cf. Carter, Brandon, "Large Number Coincidences and the Anthropic Principle in Cosmology," in *Confrontation of Cosmological Theories with Observational Data*, by Malcolm S. Longair (1974); Dyson, Freeman J., *Turbare l'Universo* (Torino, 1981). Of course, the claims cited here apply only to the (DNA- and protein-based) forms of life known to us. Theoretically, the existence of life developed in a totally different system in a different universe is also possible. After all, it is truly

All this makes it evident, again, that above the material world there is an intelligent "energy," which does not move matter in arbitrary directions, but attracts and raises it ever closer to life.

7. The boat of reason on the sea of irrationality

Human beings think, search for causes and purposes, write books, and construct machines. People seek answers in a world endowed with reason. If somebody says that life and mankind are the products of mere chance—an evolutionary error devoid of cause and purpose, he or she inevitably implies that the world lacks reason. It would seem then that the world and the events taking place in it are without cause or purpose: mankind is rowing the boat of reason on the sea of irrationality. In other words, humans are striving to understand something that has ultimately no sense and no goal, rendering the whole of human existence absurd and meaningless.[30]

We Christians do not think that reason evolved out of irrationality. Instead, we think that reason sprang from the Reason, and human logic from the *Logos*. This is how the Bible puts it: "In the beginning was the Word." (John 1:1)

As Einstein said, if someone does not believe in the Creator, they ought to expect to be faced with a chaotic world. What we are faced with is something different: we see a world with intelligent beings desiring happiness, with sensible natural and physical laws, along with a sense of morality. One could expect to find such a world if one assumed that there is an intelligent Creator.

Einstein—a non-religious person, yet a believer—also said that his discoveries of some laws or patterns in the world were among the most intense moments of his life. On such occasions, he would always feel that he was the first human in the world to have identified and understood that principle. However, he would also soon realize that the principle in question had been there since the beginning of time: Somebody had already "invented" and "implanted" it into matter. At those moments, he would feel that he had just touched the finger of the Creator and unraveled His thoughts.

---

remarkable that our world has provided an environment for an extremely fragile, vulnerable, and delicate system of life, since the beginning.
[30] Ratzinger, Joseph (Pope Benedict XVI), *Europe in the Crisis of Cultures*. Communio 32 (Summer 2005), p. 354.

8. A world open at the top

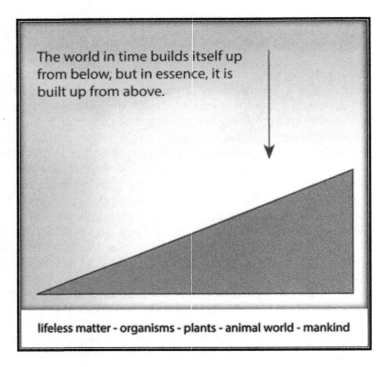

The world in time builds itself up from below, but in essence, it is built up from above.

lifeless matter - organisms - plants - animal world - mankind

All this seems to indicate that our world is "open" at the "top." Although it builds from the bottom in the course of time, with life and reason emerging slowly, in reality, the world was constructed from above. Lifeless matter, living organisms, plants, the animal kingdom and mankind—all are built from above.

Like a magnet, the power of the Creator attracts human beings to Himself through reason and through beauty.

The world is open in terms of causality.[31] This is true about its starting point, as well as about each of its intermediate points. The power of the Creator is ubiquitous in it. This also holds true for the influences induced by human activities, which far from representing simple transformations of physical matter, affect the material world substantially.

Methodologically, science may choose to refrain from exploring causes beyond physical matter but would do well to at least point to the existence of such, by way of question-raising.

---

[31] This includes not only efficient cause but also final cause.

9. "I look at Your heavens, the work of Your hands!"

Dear Reader,

Please put down the book for a moment. Look up to the sky. See the clouds, the hills, and the trees. Listen to your heart.

Philosophers such as I. Kant, S. Kierkegaard, M. Blondel, H-L. Bergson, K. T. Jaspers, P. Ricoeur, V. S. Solovyov, N. Berdyaev, and E. Lévinas, professed to be believers. Scientists such as I. Newton, W. T. Kelvin, L. Pasteur, J. A. Fleming, G. Mendel, J. C. Maxwell, A. Einstein, G. Marconi, C. G. Jung, E. Schrödinger, W. Heisenberg, M. Eigen, Abdus Salam, E. H. Erikson, V. Frankl, M. Planck, and F. O. Collins, professed to be believers.

Writers and poets such as A. Dante, L. Tolstoy, F. M. Dostoevsky, P. Claudel, G. Bernanos, T. S. Eliot, G. K. Chesterton, A. Solzhenitsyn, G. Green, S. Undset, G. Papini, A. J. Cronin, J. Milton, W. Blake, and G. Hill, professed to be believers. Statesmen such as W. Wilberforce, Martin Luther King, Dorothy Day, John F. Kennedy, A. De Gasperi, R. Schuman, and K. Adenauer, professed to be believers.

Max Planck notes, author of *Scienza, filosofia, religione*, notes that our intellect, seeking to attain a universal understanding of the world, demands that ... we identify those two forces that are replete with mystery but permeate everything: order—described by science, and God—described by the religions.[32]

---

[32] Planck, Max, *Scienza, filosofia, religione* (Milano, 1973), p. 167. It must be noted that the two mysterious forces mentioned by Planck ultimately refer to a single source: the wisdom and beauty of the Creator, manifest in the orderliness of the world.

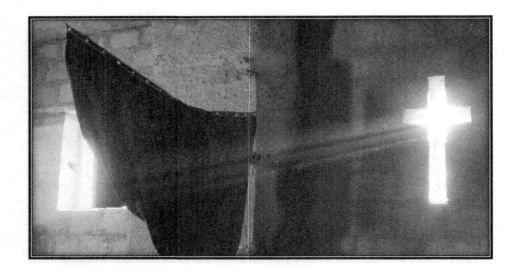

"...Aren't there people in the world who are doing things you believe are wrong—things that they should stop doing, no matter what they personally believe about the correctness of their behavior?"

Keller, Timothy, *The Reason for God: Belief in an Age of Skepticism* (London: 2009), p. 146.

III. The Moral Law in Me

1. Plato's ingenious realization

Plato speculated about the origins of the perfect and crystal-clear notions of the human mind, such as an arrow-straight line, numbers, or the images of geometric shapes. Tree trunks, for example, are twisty, so where does their inherent image of a straight line come from?

As for the ultimate perfect concept, it is that of goodness. It is never experienced in sterile form, yet people irrepressibly long for others to be good to them and yearn to be good themselves as well.

What is the source of these perfect notions arising in the human mind?[33]

Plato gives a seemingly naive, mythical answer to this question. As he relates, prior to its move to the body, the soul had seen the archetypes of the world in the divine, i.e., the divine thought, of which the material world is but a lowly reflection. This is the reason why these perfect concepts are called Platonic "ideas," an "idea" meaning something that has been seen.[34] Whatever a person can see is also already known by that person. According to Plato, when we see things here in this earthly life—"in the cave," as he puts it—we see shadows of the real divine archetypes because all earthly things partake of these. Upon seeing the shadow images, we recall the model, which we know from somewhere. We are aware that what we see resembles the real version, albeit in an imperfect way.[35]

Plato captured the essence of human exploration and the unique existential experience of mankind. Even today, this set of problems continues to represent one of the most fundamental questions of philosophy. Our exploration of finite things, along with background knowledge—traces of which are exposed in the process—constitute our peculiar self-experience.

---

[33] Cf. Plato, *The Republic*, VI. 509d – 511e; VII. 514a – 515b; Möller, J., "Idee," *Lexikon für Theologie und Kirche* (ed. J. Höfer – K. Rahner; Freiburg, 1986), pp. 602-603.

[34] The Greek noun *idéa* comes from the root *weid-, woid-, wid-* "to see." In Greek the variant *woid-* forms the verb *oîda* (*woîda* in some dialects), meaning "I know." (In form, *oîda* is a perfect tense used to show a present state: "I have seen, I know.")

[35] Cf. Plato, *The Republic*, VI, 510c – 511a.
In this section, Plato explains that the human soul, which is itself an idea, existed together with the other ideas before the creation of the world in a world of pure ideals -- the fullest ideal of all being One, i.e., "the divine." In creation, a demiurge (i.e., creator) locked up the ideals in matter, causing them to see only dimly by means of their senses. Thus, we become acquainted with the pure ideals in the material world--not through perception, but by way of recollection of the existence prior to the physical one--by partaking of the shared nature of the ideals.

2. One of the main proofs for the existence of God is man

Contemporary philosophy searches for answers to the same questions. Many philosophers and thinkers contemplate why humans perceive the tangible and visible world as finite and fragmentary. No one can ever say that they could not be even happier, or things could not be still more harmonious. No one, if they are honest with themselves, can simply resign themselves to the suffering and death of their loved ones. We just do not feel it is natural. At the bottom of our hearts, we revolt against it.

This world does not prove to be enough for a human being, whereas, for animals, it seems to be sufficient. An animal lives completely at one with the world, with its instincts exerting full control over it. A cow brilliantly knows what to do. It experiences no existential crises.

People cannot live this way. Our instincts provide us only with partial guidance as to what to do. A human being will also ask a series of questions: What is this whole thing around me about? What am I supposed to do with my life? What can I hope for? To humans, their own existence represents a problem, and they will therefore start to think.[36] It appears as though human beings fail to fit into this world by awkwardly "sticking out." They have a perspective that rises above the whole and are therefore able to ask adequate questions about it. They rise above because there is something that raises them up and makes them stand out. In other words, there is something beyond this world.

The difference between the existential experience of people and animals is evident from human speech as well. The speech of people is radically different from the sounds produced by animals. Animal sounds are direct instinct signals.[37] Sometimes they are extremely articulate, like dolphin sounds or the signals made by bees. These are direct, instinct-driven messages indicating distance, direction, danger, call, joy, etc. Human speech is completely of another kind. People conceive words such as sun, moon or star. People tend to ask: What is this? What is this whole world about? We feel we ought to understand it so that we can find our place in it. It is as if humans heard a voice from beyond the world and feel an urge to respond to this voice.[38] Therefore, people start to speak. People propose claims in their speech and attempt to define what they mean by good and right because they are convinced that truth and proper action exist, and they feel an obligation to behave accordingly.

Humans perceive this world as finite. However, the only way for us to conceive of the world as finite is by having some faint idea or trace

---

[36] Heidegger, Martin, *Being and Time* (Blackwell, Oxford, 1962), pp. 78-90.
[37] Steinvorth, Ulrich, *Was ist Vernunft? Eine philosophische Einführung* (München: 2002), p. 25. Steinworth calls this type of communication system "signal language." (*Signalsprache*).
[38] Kierkegaard, Soren, *Aut-aut* (1843).

of knowledge of completeness or perfection, and it is in relation to it that we sense our earthly experiences as finite. If nothing existed beyond this world, this world would be totally sufficient for us. We perceive it as fragmentary because we have at least a vague sense of fullness.

It is precisely this connection with reality beyond this world that is in the core of our human existence. It was this upward lifting gravitational force that once lifted mankind out of the animal world. As early Christian patristic tradition puts it: *Homo capax Dei*—A human being has an innate capacity for God.[39] People are capable of developing a sense of God and of receiving God. This is the essence of our humanity.

In other words, the ultimate proof and sign of the existence of God is the existence of this unique creature, the human being, for whom this world is not enough, and who possesses a sense and some knowledge of fullness, raising him above a finite world and himself. Karl Jaspers describes this in the following terms: "The mystery of man provides proof of the existence of God."[40]

Deep in the human spirit, there is an irrepressible sense of—and longing for—Fullness, i.e., the Creator. Stifling or ignoring this desire will make any human being ill.[41]

3. Is the concept of God a projection of our desires? The opium of the people?

According to Ludwig Feuerbach, religion is a projection of our desires. It is hard for people to tolerate the fact that they are alone in the world, and therefore they imagine a heavenly Father-God, Who cares for them. It is hard for people to tolerate earthly unhappiness, and therefore they imagine everlasting happiness in heaven, where they may be consoled. Karl Marx expressed this view even more radically when he asserted that religion—an invention of the ruling classes—was the opium administered to the people. The oppressed, suffering crowds are seen as placated with this analgesic drug, combined with a reassurance that "it will be good for you, too, in the hereafter."

How could these interpretations of religion be countered? In the

---

[39] Ratzinger, Joseph (Pope Benedict XVI), Europe in the Crisis of Cultures. Communio 32 (Summer 2005), p. 354; *Compendium of the Catechism of the Catholic Church* (2005) 1-2. *Catechism of the Catholic Church* (1993), p. 27.

[40] Jaspers, Karl, *Introduzione alla filosofia* (Milan, 2010), pp. 53-54.

[41] "(...) the chief problem of people in the middle decade of the twentieth century is emptiness. (...) Thus they feel swayed this way and that, with painful feelings of powerlessness, because they feel vacuous, empty." May, Rollo, *Man's Search for Himself* (New York, 1953), p. 24. "The typical neuroses of this age do not derive from pent-up sexuality and guilt but from the absence of orientation, norms, meaning, and reason, as well as from a sense of emptiness—in other words, from the repression of morality and religiosity." Küng, Hans, *Dio esiste?* (Milan, 1987), p. 363.

first place, it must be pointed out that Feuerbach fails to prove that God does not exist and that what religion speaks about is untrue. Instead, he postulates such, while omitting any effort to embark on any such demonstration.

What he does is pose the question: if God does not exist, how does religion nevertheless evolve in people's minds? In response to this question, he offers a quasi-psychological explanation: religion is a projection of our desires.

In objection to Feuerbach's position, it is appropriate to propose that if he thinks such an extensive system of ideas has been created out of the projection of human desires, how could it be guaranteed that his irreligiosity is not a product of the projection of his human desires? Similarly, it is possible that his atheism is only the product of his unquenchable thirst for freedom and the desire to become independent of God.

However, at a deeper level, our reaction must emphasize that it is truly remarkable we humans have this inextinguishable longing for fullness and eternity. We possess a certain type of hunger that no earthly bread may satiate. Where does this come from? There is nothing nonsensical in nature. There would be no thirst in the living world if there were no water. We would not have this unbeatable desire for fullness if that fullness did not exist and we had no sense or experience of it.

Actually, Marx's proposition is a variant of Feuerbach's idea. He similarly assumes that the realities of religion—God and the other world—do not exist. He also fails to substantiate his point, regarding religion as a pathological contrivance informed by false consciousness. What he adds to Feuerbach's concept is that, rather than evolving and thriving innocently, religion is an instrument of the ruling classes in exercising their power, the opium they administer to those living in misery so as to narcotize them and make them accept the unjust social order in which they live.

Marx's claim is valid in that religion has been used for such purposes from time to time. It has indeed become an instrument of oppression and a cover for injustice in many instances (just as art and science have been widely exploited by autocratic regimes to consolidate their own machinery of power).

Most importantly, Marx should have asked whether the claims of religion (the existence of the Creator, the concomitant, infinite dignity of mankind, etc.) are true. Communism has engendered the bloodiest totalitarian regimes in the history of humanity so far, causing unspeakable suffering and the violent deaths of over 100 million people. Is it then possible that there is something wrong with its underlying ideology, as well?

4. Are the concepts of God and morality evolutionary byproducts?

Others argue that the concepts of God and moral law are evolutionary byproducts in humans. In the past, living according to such ideas meant some advantages for the survival of an individual or group. If members of a tribe were not killing each other and helped one another, the tribe would have better chances of staying alive. This is, therefore, the source of philanthropic ethical principles.

However, this theory evades the basic questions: is it true what religion claims? Is there a Creator? Are there any moral laws and obligations? Instead, it presupposes that God does not exist, and that there are no universal moral laws. It only explains how a concept of God has developed in humans as part of evolution, not that God does not exist.

Proponents of this theory could be countered with the same objection as the one used in Feuerbach's case: if religion is a faulty evolutionary product, how can we know whether atheism is not a faulty evolutionary product, as well? After all, in the current historical phase, it could simply be more advantageous for humans from an evolutionary point of view. The real question, then, has to do with truth and how truth may be uncovered.

In essence, morality is not just a system of rules promoting survival. Although it could be arguably beneficial for a tribe if its members were not too violent with each other, this would be an insufficient criterion for morality. Instead, morality is an unconditional imperative to spare and save the life of even the enemy. Morality recognizes the rights of not only the majority, but of minorities as well. Thus, it is by no means a mere byproduct conducive to survival.[42]

5. Experiencing infinity

Above, I wrote in a slightly theoretical and philosophical manner about human beings regarding a sense of fullness. Now I would like to do the same, but in a more ordinary and easier-to-understand language.

There are moments in a person's life when he or she experiences the existence and proximity of Fullness (the Creator) through real-life events. In such a situation, the individual reaches the limits of his or her existence and potential, while experiencing that even beyond those limits, there is Something. Such an experience is called a "border experience" in philosophy.

An event of this kind could be the birth of a child, when a human being gains first-hand experience of the miracle of life. The event

---

[42] This clear and radical criterion of morality was defined by Christ and is advocated by Christianity, but every human being carries the germ of this idea in their conscience.

makes the two parents—especially the mother—realize that the little new human being was not created by them. The parents might say to themselves: "We were not able to determine even what color his or her eyes and hair would be, let alone how he or she would think and feel." A human being who had never existed before was born into this world and is starting his or her journey through life. Then a parent feels that what has happened is a miracle that far exceeds his or her capabilities. Obviously, as human beings, we have a part to play here by transmitting life. However, we do not control life, nor are we creators of life. Mankind is only a servant of life. What happens when a new human being is born into this world is well beyond our capacity.

A similar experience is when a human being loves somebody very much. There are those happy moments in marriage and romantic relationships when someone experiences that their love is not bound by reason or expectations based on reciprocity, that they would willingly give everything for the other person. When love begins to measure, it will vanish quickly. True love is always magnanimous. It is in such moments that a person in love starts to feel like *it is as though it was not even me; it is as if I had some goodness in me that is greater than I.* This is described in the Bible in the following way: "Love is of God; everyone who loves is begotten by God and knows God" (1 John 4:7). The whole world was created out of God's love. His beauty shines through the sun, the clouds, flowers, and laughing children's faces. My life also springs from this love. I will be happy only if I let this goodness flow through me as well.

Another comparable experience would be when we see or hear something captivatingly beautiful. All of sudden, we forget who and where we are. Our soul dilates into infinity.

Thus far, I have mentioned positive border experiences, when a human being reaches the limits of his or her most pleasing potential: transmitting life, loving others, and experiencing true beauty, combined with the growing awareness that there is something beyond him or her. However, negative border experiences, such as disease, aging and death, afford the same experiential potential.

Not only at the moment of death does a human being become conscious of the existence of this negative boundary, but much earlier, as well. As the Hungarian pastor and psychologist Endre Gyökössy put it, we die "in bits." People lose their prospects and health in bits and surrender their loved ones to the grave, one after another. In such situations, the individual experiences that his or her life is fading away: "I am only left with a sickbed and a handful of people to whom I still matter." If the individual is endowed with a certain amount of sensibility, this sensation will be coupled with the discovery that "although something is dying in me, there is something different that is being born inside me: I am beginning to transition into another dimension." Many dying people report that they can see the faces and hear the voices of their loved ones. There are a great many dying people who are not afraid at all in the face of death. As a young priest, I was called to minister to a dying person in a hospital in Budapest, Hungary. The ward was full of patients. The woman who had requested a priest was breathing rather heavily. When she saw me, she was gladdened and burst out saying, "Father, I am so glad you've made it here. I know that I will die soon. I've been waiting for this moment for so long. I know I am going home." The ward around her fell silent. I felt this woman was not afraid at all. It was as if she had already had one foot on the other side, as if she had seen the light awaiting her.[43]

When we believe, we believe in such experiences:[44] moments when heaven opened above us, and we came to appreciate the real depths of our existence. A person who does not believe is akin to somebody half-blind. It appears that they can only see the surface, unable to catch a glimpse of what is "beneath the veil." Faith is the sixth sense, enabling us to fathom the profundity of our existence.

---

[43] Moody, Raymond, *Life after Life* (New York, 1977). The findings of the 100 case studies conducted by Moody have since been corroborated by several research projects. Cf. Van Lommel, Pim, *Consciousness Beyond Life* (New York: 2010). A large proportion of those returning from the state of clinical death report going through the following: a sense of having died, experiencing an out-of-body state, the tunnel experience, positive sensations, the light, watching one's life quickly play out, etc. Mere physiological explanations of near-death experiences were effectively disproved *inter alios* by: Beauregard, Mario, *Brain Wars: The Scientific Battle Over the Existence of the Mind and the Proof that Will Change the Way We Live* (New York, 2012).
[44] Also, such experiences help us discover the rationality of faith.

6. The moral commandment

In effect, experience of the moral good also belongs to the category of border experiences. Nevertheless, on account of its importance, the moral good will be discussed separately.

Nowadays, many people think that there are no eternal moral norms that would be compulsory for all. They argue that morality is a product of human culture: in one society, cannibalism is an accepted form of behavior, while in another, polygamy is approved. They see morality as subjective, a function of what a particular individual or society perceives as proper, useful, or desirable.

Interestingly, however, if a most liberal person flatly rejects the existence of objective moral norms and was told that, somewhere on this planet, there is a tribe that tortures and kills some of its small children, that person would no doubt say that this practice must be discontinued, banned, and stopped from happening again— immediately. Irrespective of the culture of this community or the individual feelings of its members, such a horror can never be condoned under any circumstances.

In other words, remarkable as it may seem, every human being is fully convinced that there are objective moral norms that should be compulsory for everyone.

But from where do we get this certitude? Why are we so sure? As pointed out earlier, these norms very often represent no evolutionary asset, but rather the contrary.

Of course, regarding its details, morality may take various forms across different cultures, even individuals. That said, moral consciousness, as well as a sense of moral duty and imperative, are present in all humans. Everybody knows, at some level of being, that they should do what is good, and whatever they do not wish for themselves, they should not do to others.

When we have done something wrong, even if no one saw it and it will never come to light, there is still a voice deep in our hearts that condemns us and causes compunction. This voice cannot be silenced completely. Although it may be muffled, it is impossible to turn it off. Why is this so? Because this voice is not fully part of ourselves. We do not have total control over it. At the bottom of our hearts, we feel the light and goodness of the Creator, perceive a sense of order and harmony in the world, and see our deeds in the brightness of this shining mirror, which also makes us ashamed of every wrong choice and decision we have made.

But where does the awareness of this unconditional moral commandment in humans come from? The only possible explanation could be offered with reference to the existence of Goodness, and our cognizance of this existence.

7. Sentences with no negatives

It is intriguing to discover that there are formulations that cannot be negated meaningfully in any human language. Such an example would be: "There are eternal truths." And negating this: "There are no eternal truths," or "Truth cannot be known." Yet, should someone advance a claim like one of the above, they would also supply the refutation of their own formulation simultaneously, for if truth does not exist (or if it is beyond our reach), the sentence they just uttered cannot be true, either.

In other words, we humans are convinced that truth exists and it may be known. We are simply incapable of thinking or speaking in any other terms. Whenever we form an utterance, we do so—except for cases of deliberate lying and deception—because we deem the sentence to be true.

We are convinced that our knowledge (cognition) reaches reality and connects us with reality. We are capable of refining the truths we have come to know because we are able to compare them to reality.[45]

8. The cul-de-sac of Kant and the Enlightenment philosophers

People in antiquity may have been slightly naive in their confidence when they thought that their knowledge was objective and free from bias. They believed they saw the world as it was in reality. They conceived of cognition in the following way: sensations from the object are received by the agent through the gateway of the senses, causing the object to produce a comprehensible image or imprint in the human mind. They likened cognition to the encounter of two objects. The object leaves an imprint in the mind like a seal in wax.

Kant and the Enlightenment thinkers realized[46] that the agent is active throughout the process of cognition. What happens during cognition is not just the mere transfer of sensations from object to agent but also some kind of contribution on the agent's part to the process of cognition. To use Kant's expression, the agent projects *a priori* categories onto the object. Kant made an ingenious discovery by recognizing this truth. The agent is indeed active in the course of cognition, adding something to the process. We have seen this additional element illustrated through the color example. In the world, there are no colors detached from human or animal sight. It is

---

[45] Weissmaher, Béla, *A szellem valósága* (Budapest, 2009), pp. 135. 257.
[46] They had long been preceded in this regard by Saint Thomas Aquinas in recognizing the reality of *intellectus agens*. It was Christ and Christianity which formulated this ethical imperative in all its radicalism and clarity, but this imperative, in essence, is present in the conscience of every human being.

human and animal perception that transforms the quantitative differences between individual beams of light into qualitative differences. Kant's assertion reflects an extraordinary and groundbreaking insight.

However, Kant (and many others following in his footsteps) absolutized this insight and made it the cornerstone of all types of thinking, thus creating a distorted philosophical system and world view. What Kant proposes is that, due to the active involvement of the agent in cognition, the agent is present in all knowledge we construct. All of our knowledge is subjective (i.e., resemblant to the subject or agent) and relative (i.e., dependent on the cognizing agent). Kant's corollary of this proposition is that objective knowledge, as such, does not exist. The "thing-in-itself" (*Ding an Sich*) cannot be known. A human being may only come to know subjective representations of the "thing," i.e., its appearances. No one is in a position to know what objective truth is.

In extremely radicalized and distorted forms, the assertions of Kant and the Enlightenment thinkers have given rise to one of the tenets of contemporary, mainstream thinking, saying that truth does not exist, that there are only opinions. Some see things this way, others that way. Every view must be tolerated, and otherness needs to be respected. Each and every opinion is of equal weight and therefore weightless. Pope Benedict XVI called this world view, foisted upon the masses, the tyranny of tolerance and the dictatorship of relativism. Indeed, today's tolerant world is tolerant of everything, except for one thing: someone still having the courage to pronounce that truth exists, that it may be known, that there are moral laws, and that good is not exactly the same as bad. Such a person will be publicly discredited and dismissed as intolerant, fanatic, conservative, foolish, or fundamentalist.

Meanwhile, philosophy has negotiated the cul-de-sac that Enlightenment thinkers maneuvered themselves into. Martin Heidegger, for instance, pointed to the inappropriateness of a rigid separation between agent and object. The subject (the human being) is not an isolated bubble in the world but is part of objective reality. The meeting point in cognition is not so much about concordance between agent and object. Truth is more of an event and an act of disclosure:[47] Truth is the un-concealment of reality. As for the location where this un-concealment is most likely to occur, it is humankind. Thus, Heidegger calls a human *Dasein* or "being there." It is in human beings that Existence is present, speaks, and is disclosed. In other words, what Heidegger demonstrates is that the place where objective truth (i.e., reality) most typically appears is in human beings,

---

[47] Primary meaning of the Greek word *aletheia* (= truth): unconcealed, revealed. Cf. Heidegger, Martin, *Being and Time* (Blackwell, Oxford, 1962) pp. 256-273.

themselves, i.e., in the subject. What is most subjective or most authentically human is also most objective. What this world is about, and who mankind is, is most profoundly revealed not by scientists' test tubes, but through Mozart's Requiem or Michelangelo's Pietà. It is through Man that Existence speaks.

Of course, truth does not speak in an authentic voice through every human being; truth is spoken only through those who live an authentic life. Such people do not do or say what is conventionally done or said,[48] but embrace the true potential and challenge of their existence. Along these lines, Heidegger argues that the primary job of philosophy is to search for those personalities, moments, and phenomena in the past through which Existence spoke and was disclosed. At this point, Heidegger approximates to the view held by Christianity,[49] claiming that God (the objective Truth and Reality) has manifested and revealed Himself through individuals in history.

All this begs the question of how long it will take humanity to become aware of the untenability of the cul-de-sac of Enlightenment and finally navigate its way out of it.

9. Does all this amount to proof?

At the end of this chapter, the question seems almost inevitable: does this all provide proof for the existence of the Creator and the meaning of life?

At this juncture, it is important to consider what it is that may be regarded as evidence. Modern science has established measurement and empirical validity as the only accepted and methodologically appropriate manner of evidence collection. Given its highly specialized academic standards, this is not necessarily a problem.

With this method, however, it is only possible to treat issues that are inconsequential from the point of view of existence.[50] Existence is multilayered. The fact that Mozart's Requiem is aesthetically pleasing appears to be evident, yet instruments of specialized science cannot prove it. Nevertheless, this aesthetic quality is real and existent. The fact that a husband loves his wife cannot be determined from his blood sample and does not lend itself to measurement, yet it is real. It represents such a powerful reality that moves human lives and our history. It is not only the countable and the tangible that exists.

Pope Benedict XVI called the acceptance of only empirically measurable aspects as relevant, the arbitrary self-imposed limitation

---

[48] Heidegger applies the following label to identify this mode of existence: *Das Man* (= "the 'they'", i.e., Man in general); cf. Heidegger, Martin, *Being and Time* (Blackwell, Oxford, 1962), p. 297.

[49] Though Heidegger, himself, does not talk about the revelation of God but rather the silence of God.

[50] Nichols, Aidan, *La pensée de Benoit XVI* (Geneva, 2008) p. 363.

of reason. What an impoverished world evolves out of such an understanding of reality!

When facing an individual and deciding whether to believe in or like him or her, we do not have incontrovertible empirical measurement results at our disposal. God represents a kind of Reality that cannot be measured by instruments, that does not exist on our level of existence, and that we do not "bump into" in our visible and tangible world, as we would a piece of furniture. He is a Person (albeit in a completely different sense from a human person) and a Mystery, of Whom we perceive, and of Whom the world and the human heart furnish a variety of hints. He is knocking on your door. You cannot spare yourself the decision whether to open the door to Him.

The following story happened in the United States. A boy was fond of playing baseball but was not a particularly good player, so he was never selected for major matches. However, there was something unique about this young man: he loved his father very much. His father frequently came to meet him at the end of practices. On such occasions, the boy would leave everything behind, run to his father and hug him. Next to the field, there was a park, where they would take a walk, holding hands. It was apparent that the relationship between father and son was a truly special one. Then the boy's father died. The coach asked in desperation, "How is this kid going to go on living?" The boy was absent from practices for a long time but eventually turned up one day. When the practice was over, he went up to the coach and said to him, "This Saturday, we are having an important match. Please put me on the starting team, sir." Initially reluctant to comply as the boy really was not a good player, the coach finally consented to the request out of respect for the grief of the boy. Arriving home, in retrospect, he regretted his leniency. However, on Saturday, the boy was indeed standing in the starting lineup and played like magic. All of his hits were precise, and he ran so fast that no one could get close to him. Far from wanting to replace him during the match, the coach ran up to him at the end and asked him, "What's happened to you? You've never played like this before!" The boy replied, "You know, sir, this was because of my dad. I'm not sure whether you noticed it, but he was completely blind. This was my first match that he could see. I was playing for him."[51]

When we know that there is Someone Who watches us with infinite love: our Creator, to Whom we will one day go home, we will play the game of our life better, with fewer inhibitions and more generosity.

[51] *Illustrations Unlimited: A Topical Collection of Hundreds of Stories, Quotations, & Humor,* ed. James S. Hewett (Tyndale House Publishers, 1988), p. 171.

IV. A Good God and a Bad World?

I Will Praise the Lord of Wisdom
(an ancient Akkadian poem)

Oh that my vexation were weighed,
and all my calamity laid in the balances!
For then it would be heavier than the sand of the sea;
For the arrows of the Almighty are in me;
my spirit drinks their poison;
the terrors of God are arrayed against me.
Oh that I might have my request, and that God would fulfill
my hope, that it would please God to crush me, that he would
let loose his hand and cut me off!
This would be my comfort ... (...)
The poor of the earth all hide themselves.
Behold, like wild donkeys in the desert
the poor go out to their toil, seeking game;
the wasteland yields food for their children.
They go about naked, without clothing;
hungry, they carry the sheaves (...)

From out of the city the dying groan,
and the soul of the wounded cries for help;
yet God charges no one with wrong ... (Job 6:2-10; 24:4-12)

I look about me; evil upon evil!
My affliction increases, right I cannot find.
I implored the god, but he did not turn his countenance;
I prayed to my goddess, but she did not raise her head (...)
What bizarre actions everywhere! I looked behind:
persecution, harassment! [52]

---

[52] An Akkadian poem. Pritchard, James B., *Ancient Near Eastern Texts: Relating to the Old Testament* (Princeton University Press: 1969), p. 434.

The Nobel laureate and Holocaust survivor, Elie Wiesel, relates an incident in Auschwitz involving the hanging of two men and a young boy. All of the barrack inmates were forced to witness the executions. The two men died quickly, but the boy's death agony lasted a good half an hour. As they saw the small body writhing on the rope, the terrible silence was broken by the woeful cry of one of the prisoners: "Where is God?" And he heard a voice in his heart with a reply: "Where is He? He is there ... over there, on the gallows."[53]

To the question, "Why is there suffering?", the answers proposed here are only tentative and incomplete responses. When faced with the mystery of suffering, first and foremost, we should pause and keep quiet, with compassion in our hearts and a helping hand extended to those in need. The answer God offers to the question of suffering is not a theoretical one: His response is essentially Jesus's Cross and Resurrection.

In this chapter, several points are introduced, including the Person of Jesus, His divinity, and belief in eternal life—themes that will be discussed and put into perspective in subsequent sections.

1. Why does the question come up?

In order to pose a meaningful question on suffering (eg., Why do bad things happen in the world?), the one asking must be ready to accept the possibility that God exists and He is a merciful and just Creator. If the world is only an arena governed by blind chance, why should we expect it to be merciful to us? It is only natural that it should be blind and merciless. The problem of suffering only makes sense if we accept the possibility that there is a good and just Force behind the world, providing grounds for our hopes for a better one and a better personal fate than what we experience. Thus, indirectly, even a question targeting the *bad* suggests that we are cognizant of the Creator and we expect a better world from Him.[54]

2. The moral bad

The "bad" present in our world may be divided into two main types: the physical bad and the moral bad. The category "physical bad" includes diseases, natural catastrophes, and death. The category "moral bad" could refer to anything that stems from the wrong actions of people: hatred, families falling apart, wars, the misery of the

---

[53] Hoffsümmer, Willi, *Kurzgeschichten, Bd. 1* (Mainz, 1995), p. 41.
[54] Cf. Lewis, C.S., *Mere Christianity* (New York, 1960) p. 31; Plantinga, Alvin, "A Christian Life Partly Lived," *Philosophers, Who Believe: The Spiritual Journeys of 11 Leading Thinkers* (ed. Clark, Kelly James; 1993) p. 73; Keller, Tim, *The Reason for God: Belief in an Age of Skepticism* (London, 2009) pp. 25-27.

poor, etc. The scope of the moral bad is much broader than we would initially imagine. For instance, the privations of the African Continent are not the result of a natural disaster. Africa has been exploited a million times: millions of slaves were carried away from the continent, it was colonized and state borders were drawn in a completely arbitrary fashion with no regard for ethnic or historical reality, the bulk of its minerals and natural resources continue to be kept under external control to the present day, and so forth. Of course, the causes of Africa's suffering also include the countless corrupt and ruthless dictators and leaders who are all too frequently supplied with weapons and kept in power by western interest groups. Therefore, it is obvious that Africa's poverty is by no means the consequence of some accidental natural calamities; the continent's misery has primarily been induced by innumerable human sins.

Similarly, a large proportion of illnesses are also due to human sins and the disharmony they entail. Medical science is beginning to appreciate how many diseases have psychological roots. It seems that a large number of illnesses—from hypertension to diabetes, gastric and cardiac diseases, even some forms of cancer—are caused by spiritual disharmony. Subsequently, many of these diseases or related susceptibility to them may be passed on to future generations.

Thus, it appears that the moral bad encompasses a rather wide spectrum of what is bad in the world. It predominantly represents those things that make human life bitter and unhappy: the malice of others, absence of love in the family, as well as experiences of human cruelty and injustice. These are not brought about by God, the Creator, but by humankind. Here, God is not to be blamed or held responsible.

Naturally, however, the question whether God could have created a world in which human beings would not be able to do evil is a justifiable one. Theoretically, it is possible to conceive of a world where no evil act could be done, with everything and everybody operating perfectly, like well-oiled machines. Such a world would be free from anything bad, but equally, it would have nothing truly good in it either—not even a snippet of joy or a shred of love, art, or happiness. This is because the happiness of human beings is enabled precisely by their ability to experience that someone loves them (or they love someone), not because of an inability to do otherwise, owing to some prior programming, but the ability to do so voluntarily, out of their own free will—even if, at times, this love comes at a price. God is Love, and He has created a world in which people are capable of giving love. This world, however, also offers freedom, along with the possibility of misusing that freedom.

3. The physical bad

From the point of view of faith in God, a weightier problem is represented by the existence of the physical bad. The cause of the physical bad is simply the finiteness and perishability of the material world and the vulnerability of living organisms. All this does not come from human sin, since volcanoes erupted and meteors hit the Earth, with living organisms indiscriminately destroyed in the wake of such catastrophes, well before the appearance of humans. Diseases also pre-dated the appearance of humans (for example, paleontologists have found cancerous dinosaur bones), and death had also existed before the arrival of humans. (In other words, without the death of living beings, evolution itself would not be possible, either.)

These negative aspects are but the consequence of the finiteness, vulnerability, and perishability of matter. The Creator does not control protons and electrons through invisible strings. He gave a certain degree of "liberty" to the material world, as well.[55] There is consensus among physicists that, even if we know everything about the material world at the present moment, the processes that are to take place tomorrow, or in the next moment, cannot be predicted with full certainty.[56] It seems that a tiny seed of freedom is already present in matter.

God did not create things in the world in a ready-made form. He called life into being and let life itself discover its more noble forms on a long road full of cul-de-sacs and suffering. He does not make people ready, either. He allows us to be involved in the process of composing our life journeys, and in the construction of our very selves. He intended the human being to be His true companion. "Liberty" in the material world is a prerequisite of freedom in the world of humans.[57]

---

[55] As rabbis put it, God "takes a step back" at the time of creation so that He may give way to the world, to something that is different from Him. God wills the world to be relatively independent, autonomous and free. Cf. Jonas, Hans, *Il concetto di Dio dopo Auschwitz* (Genova, 1989). This "freedom" of matter may also be called the potential for self-determination.

[56] This is implied by Heisenberg's uncertainty relation, and it is also suggested by a series of experiments. As part of these tests, radiation was sent into a cloud chamber through two slots. From the experiments, it appeared as though the rays enjoyed some freedom as to how to behave. The behavior of each ray could only be predicted statistically. It was on account of such observations that modern physics finally abandoned the deterministic understanding of matter. Matter does not work like a pre-programmed clockwork mechanism. Cf. Heisenberg, Werner, *Physics and Philosophy: The Revolution in Modern Science* (Penguin Books, London, 1990), pp. 7-14, 67-76.

[57] "(...) genuine randomness is a pre-condition of real human freedom. That a law of averages requires that some shall suffer is small comfort to the one who suffers. True though this is, suffering can be aggravated by the belief that it has been deliberately inflicted." Bartholomew, D. J., *God of Chance* (SCM Press Ltd, London, 1984), p. 157. Jesus firmly rejects the notion that particular instances of suffering could be God's punishment for particular sins (cf. Luke 13:1-5; John 9:3).

Experiencing the physical bad is not inherently bad. The physical bad (e.g., diseases, catastrophes, death) confronts us with the fact that we are finite and nothing more than a creature. Instances of the physical bad make us face the limits of our being and the truths of our existence.

Pain is an important indication for living beings, signaling illness or injury. Adversity and suffering have been the engine of the development of the living world and humankind.[58]

The physical bad is so painful for mankind because he has been wounded by sin. And a sinful man does not trust his Creator with all his heart and does not fully believe in the reality of eternal life. Therefore, he clings onto his finite earthly life and his health tenaciously, experiencing illness and death as bitter anguish and agony. For a sinful man, illness and death are inevitably painful, though these could have ensured a natural and hopeful transition into God's eternal presence.

It was both shocking and uplifting for myself and others to witness the death of an old Salesian brother in the Salesian monastery situated in the fertile valley of Cremisan, overlooking Bethlehem in Palestine. Everyone could go up to his sickbed, and he would smile at each of them, sometimes even speaking a few words to them. He died with a smile on his face in peace. When he passed, I felt that he had reached his home. The monastery was filled with a mystical air of heavenly peace.

---

[58] Cf. Martinetti, Giovanni, *Perché credo nella vita eterna* (Torino, 2001), p. 112.

4. Mohamed's answer to the question of suffering

Now let us consider briefly what two of the world's principal religions, Islam and Buddhism, say about the meaning of suffering. Mohamed does not attach any special explanation to suffering. What he teaches is that Allah's will must simply be accepted.[59]

It is by no means a rare occurrence that a young woman sits at her husband's sickbed in a hospital, and when her husband dies, she rises without uttering a word of grief and says that this was Allah's will, accepting this pain with immense faith.

There is something captivating and powerful in this conduct: strong faith without asking or complaining. At the same time, there is also something alarming in it: it is as if human questions disappear together with the chance to think, inevitably suggesting that a human being is only supposed to show blind obedience.

5. Buddha's answer to the question of suffering

As indicated by the biographical data available, Siddhārtha Gautama[60] was born into a prominent family in the Shakya clan around 558 BC. He lived a rich and carefree life in a magnificent palace surrounded by walls. He had a wife and son at the time when he stepped outside the ornamental garden of the palace and witnessed a sick man, an old man, and a corpse—old age, illness, and death. He left the palace behind, moved to the woods, and began searching for answers to the question of suffering, leading the life of a hermit. Seven years later, while sitting under a tree, he attained "enlightenment," an event that would subsequently bestow the name Buddha, i.e., "the Awakened One," upon him.

What did the Buddha awaken to? He encapsulated the main message of his enlightenment as four noble truths. The Buddha claimed that, in human life, everything is suffering (*dukkha*), and suffering is caused by desire and craving for existence (*taṇhā*). Human beings excessively yearn for riches, health, beauty, and love from others, however this thirst is not fully satiated, so this is what constitutes the root of human suffering. The Buddha proposed that the solution is the extinction of craving for existence (*taṇhā khaya*) and the eradication of desires. Excessive desire for anything is to be avoided so that nothing may be taken away from the individual.[61]

---

[59] Cf. Quran 2:154-156; 21:23.
[60] The Buddha's life is surrounded by many uncertainties because the surviving records on him were written approx. 400 years after his death. Cf. Eliade, Mircea, *A History of Religious Ideas, vol. II* (University of Chicago Press, Chicago, IL, 1982). pp. 74-89; De Rosa, Giuseppe, *Cristianesimo, religioni e sette non cristiane a confronto* (Rome, 1994), pp. 130-149.

[61] Cf. ed. Ghislandi C., *Buddhismo* (Bologna, 1975), p. 19.

There is some truth to this. Perhaps, it is us westerners, in particular, who ought to heed the Buddha's words. Individuals living in the western world frequently appear to be incapable of accepting the world and themselves as they are. They tend to overstretch themselves in their effort to transform everything according to their own ideas and desires. They build highways right across the globe and transform even their own bodies. On the contrary, the Buddha tells you to calm down. The world is as good as it gets, and you are fine the way you are. Take a seat under the tree and blend into primeval harmony. This is what happiness consists of.

There is, however, a fundamental error in the Buddha's proposition. His basic question is, What do I need to do so that I will not suffer? In order for us to achieve this state, he suggests that we eradicate our desires. We are not supposed to be concerned about what is happening around us, or whether we are loved or not. This way, a human being actually cuts his or her ties with the world and sacrifices his or her ability to love.

When in 1948, Saint Mother Theresa of Calcutta walked the streets of Calcutta (Kolkata, India), she was met with the sight of the infirm suffering from various diseases and the dying lying on the streets completely abandoned. People were simply stepping over them. This attitude could be accounted for by a general sense of inability to offer meaningful help, as well as by the conviction that everyone has their own destiny, which must be accepted: "This is their fate, and I have my own, so we have nothing to do with each other." People thinking this way literally cut the ties connecting them with the outside world.[62] Mother Teresa was unable to go past the dying. The first person she raised from the ground was a woman of around forty years of age, whose feet the rats had started to feed on. Even though the

---

[62] It goes without saying that this context is dominated by Hindus and not Buddhists. Compassion is a central element of Buddhist teaching. Nevertheless, with regard to fundamental beliefs, the two religions show some resemblance, including aspects of the doctrine of reincarnation.

woman was still alive, she was not in a condition to defend herself. Mother Theresa picked her up and took her to several hospitals, only to find that they were turned down everywhere on the grounds that hospitals were not supposed to admit the dead. And this woman was still alive! In the end, she died in Mother Theresa's arms on the street. It was at that moment that she decided she would make a house for the dying in Calcutta.

The Buddha's teaching is also informed by a certain world view. Like the majority of eastern thinkers, the Buddha is also a believer in reincarnation. But what is the doctrine of reincarnation really about? It basically asserts that individual human beings are, after all, insignificant. Every human life is but a tiny moving part in the history of a particular soul—one day it goes by the name of Jennifer Smith, and the next it is known as John Jackson. Whatever is personal in them, including their memories and relationships of love, tying them to their parents, family, and friends, will all be gone and dismissed as inconsequential. No one is interested in any of this, least of all the "god," or ultimate goal, of having no self. The Buddha never actually says that God loves us. He regards this as an outright absurd assertion. There is no strand in his thought that would link the divine to individual persons. Finally, even this "spiritual brook" of changing lives ceases to exist, assimilating into the eternal ocean of the nothingness, and desires along with consciousness are extinguished in nirvana. The terminal state is annihilation.[63] On this final stage, i.e., the Absolute, Buddhism remains humbly silent, as it denotes a form of existence that transcends the bounds of earthly existence. Buddhism does not define this state in positive terms, though, at times, it goes as far as to describe this as "happiness."

One of the basic tenets of Buddhism is the denial of the self (*anatta*). Craving for existence originates in the self. Buddhism sees the finite earthly world as negative and strives to break free from it. Through its claim about the irrationality of the self, it seeks to eradicate selfishness.[64] Christianity, on the contrary, views this finite, earthly life as God's gift and masterpiece, permeated by His presence, and something that must be cherished and enriched by mankind. The goal is not to eliminate the self but to realize its full potential in

---

[63] "In this nothingness framework, nirvana means extinguishing the self so completely that the illusion of reality has no more impact. The word nirvana comes from combining the Sanskrit past participle /*ban*/ "blown" and the adverb /*nis*/ "out, away." It originally meant nothing more than what one does to a candle's flame. And while there were other words circulating at the Buddha's time for liberation from rebirth (*moksha, mukti, samadhi*), the word nirvana was deliberately chosen by the Buddha to convey this puff-and-your-gone release from the illusion of reality (*maya*). No soul, no universe, just nothingness." Cf. "Nirvana in Buddhism: Definition & Methods," study.com, https://study.com/learn/lesson/what-is-nirvana-in-buddhism.html, accessed July 7, 2023.
[64] Eliade, Mircea, *A History of Religious Ideas, vol. II* (University of Chicago Press, Chicago, IL, 1982), p. 78.

love.

The worldview of Buddhism is a pessimistic one.[65] This is why the Buddha proclaims that we must sever our ties with the world outside. It is as though he is saying, "Anyway, you will lose everything in the end. Therefore, make sure to spare yourself the pain of loss well in advance." This implies a sense of calm indeed, the calm of death: a death that has been executed in advance.[66]

6. The moral teaching of the Buddha

At the same, it must be acknowledged that the Buddha provided his followers with some absolutely noble and praiseworthy moral guidelines. The ten great precepts are as follows: refrain from taking life of all forms and turn to others with loving kindness; refrain from appropriating whatever has not been given to you and be generous to others; abstain from all manner of sexual misconduct and practice forbearance; refrain from lying, obscene and evil talk, base calumnies, as well as from thoughtless and foolish prattle. Instead, speak in truth with kindness and politeness, in the spirit of consensus and helpfulness at all times; avoid covetousness and ensure peace of mind; desist from malice and be sympathetic to others; lastly, abandon your misconceptions and progress in the pursuit of wisdom.[67] Buddhist teachers of later periods would deliver their teachings along the following lines: *Patient endurance is the highest form of asceticism; No true "goer forth" is he who injures another, nor is he a samana[68] who causes harm to others;* and *Refraining from evil, undertaking the good, purifying one's mind—this is the disposition of the Buddhas.*[69]

Buddhism abounds in remarkable teachings and saintly paragons of humaneness, meekness, and meditation. I mean to complement my previous critical statements with this key addition, as well as to call on the followers of the Buddha's teaching to learn from Christ, the Man of Sorrows, by considering His truly divine answer to suffering.

---

[65] Cf., De Rosa, Guiseppe, *Cristianesimo, religioni e sette non cristiane a confronto* (Rome, 1994), pp. 139-141. Naturally, this does not preclude the *joie de vivre* and life-affirmation of Buddhism.

[66] My comments concern abstract doctrine exclusively. In writing these critical lines, I never mean to pass judgment on the adherents of Buddhism (or of Hinduism, Taoism, etc.), or even on the Buddha himself. Followers of Buddhism and of other eastern religions are often considerably more humane and loving than many Christians. The true image and law of God is written on the human heart, and therefore believers of other religions may as well possess a clear image of God, sometimes even at odds with the doctrines of their own religions, and lead exemplary lives in accordance with that image.

[67] Skilton, Andrew, *A Concise History of Buddhism* (Windhorse Publications Ltd., Cambridge, UK, 1994), pp. 33-34.

[68] A Buddhist ascetic contemplative

[69] Ibid. 35.

7. Jesus and suffering

Jesus understands the meaning of life differently from Buddha. Jesus's most fundamental question is not, *What do I need to do so that I will not suffer?* His basic question is, *What do I need to do so that I may love?* The world has been created out of love, and human beings reach their full potential if they love and dedicate their lives to others. Jesus assures us that we need not be afraid when we see that this love comes at a price, requiring us to relinquish parts of ourselves at times, for to love also means to become one with others and carry their burdens. It is thus for a reason that the chief symbol of Christianity is not a smiling Buddha facing the immeasurable suffering of the world with equanimity, but the Cross, and a divine face filled with blood and tears—the face of God, Who loves us passionately.

What Jesus teaches us is not that we should stifle our desires and cut the ties that connect us to the world. In fact, He encourages us to relate to and love one another. For instance, He exalts the matrimonial bond and speaks of it as divine because nothing will perish but will come to fulfillment. This is a radically optimistic worldview. Jesus teaches that every single human being is infinitely important to God. The bond of love links God to us, inseparably. The names of individual human beings are written on God's Name (cf. Luke 20:37-38).

8. God suffered: He is one with us in suffering

Christianity makes such shocking pronouncements, such as God assuming our mortal nature, suffering, and dying for us. Jesus's Cross revealed to us the innermost mystery of God, the heart of the Creator in history.

God's every deed is eternal. Jesus's Cross declares that God is not watching humanity's enormous suffering from the comfort of a distant, celestial palace. Along the ongoing *Via Crucis* (literally, the "Way of the Cross") of history, God has taken our burdens upon Himself and carried our pain. And with His resurrection, He has defeated suffering and death.

When someone suffers, God is there with them and becomes one with them. At such times, the individual experiences the mysteries of Good Friday and Easter.

9. We live in order to learn to love

The world was made from the love of the Creator. The Creator's goodness and beauty shine through the radiance of the sun, the singing of birds, the brooks and the clouds. Human existence also sprang from this love. The Creator wants us to reach His everlasting love and intends that our lives will be fulfilled in union with Him.

This earthly life is transitory. It is meant to enable us to gradually learn to take control of ourselves, to learn individual decision-making, and then to learn to love and surrender our lives. Initially, we surrender our lives in small ways—through work, our families, and those entrusted to our care—until in the ultimate, great gesture of faith and love, we commit ourselves into the hands of God, wholly and finally.

Only once we have learned to love in this earthly, transitory existence, can we enter God's eternal love. This is the goal of our journey on earth.

A famous tale[70] relates that a little boy once heard an amazing tune in his heart. It was pleasing and captivating, like the view of the first blue sky in spring and the babbling of a mountain stream. When the little boy became aware of it, he said to himself, "This is so beautiful that I will take it to the Lord and give it to Him." And he did, indeed, take that melody to the Lord.

The Lord listened to the music with delight and said He was pleased with the music of the boy's life: "This is truly amazing," said God. "If you'd like, I will help you to make it perfect." And He gave the boy love.

The little boy grew and matured, and the tune in his heart changed in the meanwhile: it became imbued with emotions and depth. When he heard it in its new form, he thought it was complete and took it to the Lord again. As before, God was overjoyed to listen to it, but eventually said, "Something is still missing from it." And He presented the man with suffering.

The man struggled and rebelled. Oftentimes, he felt he could not bear it any longer, fearing he would be crushed by the suffering and lose his faith. But then he slowly overcame and defeated it. In the meantime, the tune also changed a little in his heart. A deep, melancholic base tone was added to it. But this made it only more sonorous and more triumphant. When the man heard it, he took it to the Lord and said to Him, "Everything that I had, I put into this melody. I wrote it with the blood of my heart. I have nothing else that I could give to You. Please accept it."

But God said, "I have one more gift for you." And He presented the man with loneliness.

The sounds of the world gradually faded around the man. As he

[70] Hoffsümmer, Willi, *Kurzgeschichten* 3 (Mainz, 1987), pp. 114-115.

fought his way through the bitterness and grace of loneliness, the tune changed a little in his heart again. It became more and more spiritual and transparent. When the Lord heard it, deeply touched in His heart, He accepted it.

We all learn the tune of a lifetime of love, in the often difficult school of life. And to advance from one form of love to another in this school, sometimes we must complete extremely painful journeys.

As C. S. Lewis said, "God whispers through our joys, speaks intelligibly through the voice of our conscience, and shouts aloud through our suffering."[71] Dietrich Bonhoeffer, a pastor of great faith, executed by the Nazis, wrote that suffering is a holy angel. It induced more good in people than any amount of indulgence or pleasure.[72] The human heart is often hard. Suffering breaks this hard cover and opens the heart to God and one's fellow human beings. It can make us humbler and more compassionate. In suffering, we can come to experience the truths of our existence and our finiteness. It can lead us to God, the Source of Existence.

The Bible teaches us that, in our sufferings, we complete the redemptive Passion of Christ (Col. 1:24). Every affliction that we bear with faith and love renders us like Christ. We carry the burden of the world together with Him, and through our love, we can participate in the work of purification from sins and salvation.

10. Where is my Father?

One of the great sufferers of the Bible is Job, the righteous man, who suffered innocently. Job called out to God and demanded an answer from Him. Actually, the meaning (or at least one of the possible interpretations) of Job's name is "Where is my Father?"[73] Job searches for the loving God in the night of suffering. A sufferer is allowed to cry, complain, and argue with God.

God responded to Job's plea in Christ's Cross:[74] "Here I am. I am with you! You have a Father. You walk the hard paths of suffering with me." The road of suffering leads to the light of the Resurrection.

Francis S. Collins, a leading scientist of the Human Genome Project, had been an agnostic as a young man and subsequently an atheist for many years. Then he decided to go to medical school. At his patients'

---

[71] Lewis, C.S., *The Problem of Pain* (New York, 1996), p. 91.
[72] Cf. Peppin, Bruce, *The Best Is Yet to Be: Moving Mountains in Midlife* (Colorado Springs, 2015), pp. 184-185. Dietrich Bonhoeffer wrote this in a letter from 1944.
[73] The original meaning of the name of Job is uncertain. Some construe it as "enemy" with reference to the wordplay in Job 13:24. However, based on Mesopotamian parallels, the meaning "Where is my Father?" appears to be more plausible. Cf. STEINMANN, J., *Le livre de Job* (Paris, 1955), p. 77; Pope, M.H., "Job, Book of," *The Interpreter's Dictionary of the Bible*, vol. 2 (Nashville, 1986), p. 911; Crenshaw, James, L., "Job, Book of," *The Anchor Bible Dictionary*, vol. 3 (New York, 1992), p. 858.
[74] Cf. Jung, Carl Gustav, *Antwort auf Hiob* (Zurich, 1952).

sickbeds, he was moved by the relationships that developed between him and the dying patients. He was touched by the strength that sprang from their faith. He understood that, not being part of the physical universe, God cannot be approached with the help of the experimental methods of natural sciences. Yet God speaks to us. He calls us to help others, even if we don't expect anything in return. This altruism, as Collins says, challenges the vital principles associated with the "selfish gene," the competition based on self-centeredness. Collins became a believer.[75]

Some years ago, I had the opportunity to accompany a married couple through an extremely difficult period of their lives. The wife, a young and buoyant mother of five, was diagnosed with a rare and incurable disease, causing her neurons to die gradually. At first, she only noticed that some words would escape her, and her movements were becoming increasingly harder. Before long, she was confined to a wheelchair, and finally was bedridden.

Her husband would frequently ask God, "Why? Why does a vigorous, cheerful, and devoutly religious mother need to go through this horrible ordeal?" And then—as he told me—he was led to realize that he was not supposed to ask this question. He intuitively felt that he might come to appreciate the reason only in the hereafter, when he could see the world and life through the eyes of God. For now, however, it was sufficient for him to know that God was with them—and they were able to feel this almost physically. Without that, they could not have seen a single day, or even a single hour, through.

The woman's condition was deteriorating. She became completely unable to speak. She could only move her eyes and face to some extent. The husband learned to read his wife's look. Then the wife's condition worsened further; she was taken to the hospital, placed on life support, and fed through a stomach tube, as she wasn't able to swallow. However, in the hospital, no one could read the woman's look; they failed to make sense of her infinitesimal signals. Her psychological condition quickly declined, as well. At one point, the husband made a major decision. He was determined to bring his wife home. He purchased a life support machine and studied everything that was necessary so that he could attend to all the needs of his wife. He gave up his excellent job and cared for his wife, alone, twenty-four hours a day, for more than two years. On some nights, he would get up twenty or thirty times to take care of her. His wife had a little bell that she was able to press with one finger still capable of making some limited movements. She was often scared, feeling unable to breathe, and would wake up her husband. Many people would ask the man why he was doing this, and he would always reply, "Isn't it

[75] Collins, Francis S., *The Language of God. A Scientist Presents Evidence for Belief* (New York, 2006).

only natural? I am glad that I can do at least this much for her. I am sure she would be doing the same for me."

On their last Christmas together, we celebrated Mass by her sickbed. Their five children and the husband were kneeling around the bed. As we walked out of the sickroom, the man said to me, "Father, you know, this room is very special for us. Here, we are covered by the veil of God's love."

The Grafting-Knife of God
by Árpád Tóth

Money, health, and success,
To others, Lord, you have given more.
I will not sue for it, nonetheless,
Nor say you are my debtor.
I'm not your first stepchild.
Your knife of trials between my ribs I bless.
I smile at fools whose woes bring anger wild,
Who beat themselves vainly upon the chest.
I've known and felt your love from the start:
The grafting knife of your afflictions is in me,
It serves you, for while it injures my heart,
The wounding brings new beauty.
I clench my lips when pain is hard to bear,
Because I know the battles I fight are yours,
and into the far-off victory I stare
My face, fair with tears,
and thy cheek bright.[76]

---

[76] Translation by Christine Watkins

V. To Believe in One Concrete Religion: Folly and Narrow-mindedness?

According to an ancient story of Indian origin,[77] a maharajah[78] once had some blind people touch an elephant. After they touched it, he asked them what the elephant was like. One after the other, they gave their responses, such as, "It is like a bowl" (the head), "It is like a soft basket" (the ears), "It is like a plowshare" (the tusk), "like a plow" (the trunk), "like a granary" (the belly), "like a pillar" (the legs), "like a mortar" (the back), "like a pestle" (the tail) or "like a brush" (the hairy tip of the tail). The blind people began to quarrel and ended up fighting each other.

The Buddha taught that religions can be likened to these people. They each perceived or laid their hands on fragments of the divine, the mystery of life, which is incomprehensible in its entirety. Everything would have been fine if they had conceded that their knowledge was but fragmentary. The situation became problematic when they absolutized their teachings and assailed one another.

Others compare religions to a variety of roads leading up to the top of a single mountain. It seems obvious that there is only one deity—whether He is called Allah, Deus, God, or Shiva. Every religion represents a path to the peak. Even though one might appear to run in a straight line, while another could look slightly twisted, they are essentially all equivalent.

Others think that the demand of some religions for exclusivity is a sign of arrogance and intolerance, constituting one of the major problems of human history. They argue that all religions claiming exclusivity should be obliterated, or at a minimum, such views should be prohibited from becoming vocal in the public domain.

Yet others point out that each religion is culture dependent. In their opinion, it would be foolish to designate any particular religion as the repository of the whole truth.[79]

1. What is religion?

We, Christians, believe that, in essence, religion is not about human beings' search for God and their attempt to encounter Him. Religion does not consist in a person trying to rise to Him by climbing up a metaphorical hill.

The main issue in true religion, as well as in the history of humankind, is not that we searched for God, but that He searched for us. The point in true religion is not that we strive to clamber up to Him, but that He has descended to us.

[77] Here, the ancient tale is presented in the version employed by the Buddha, cf. The Udana 6:4-6.
[78] Sanskrit title for great king
[79] Cf. Keller, Timothy, The Reason for God (London, 2009), pp. 9-11.

2. God had to descend to our level of existence

Entities in the world exist at different levels of existence: inanimate objects, plants, animals, humans, and God.[80] Jumping from one level up to the next one is not possible. A stone will not sprout by itself, nor will a plant see or hear. By the same token, an animal is rather unlikely to appreciate whatever is human in a human being. If I am reading poems by William Everson, and a little mouse comes up to my feet, it will never be able to comprehend what I am doing, as it lacks the necessary senses.

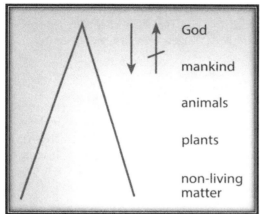

God

mankind

animals

plants

non-living matter

Similarly, humans are also incapable of perceiving or experiencing God as He is. Although He is present everywhere (even in the very place where you are reading the pages of this book), and His presence is more real than anything else, we cannot experience Him in His own reality. He is at a different level of existence.

If God wants us to be able to experience, comprehend, and receive Him, as well as to be in union with Him, He must descend to our level. He must give a sign of Himself in space and time.

3. God is a Person

There are many who believe that the divine is a kind of energy: an infinite power and impersonal wisdom. Others endow matter itself with these mysterious properties.

Christianity (along with many other religions) is defined by the conviction that God is a Person. Why do we hold this to be true? In the world, which sprang from the Creator, there are persons, there are individuals. In it, there is the human being with free will, consciousness, and the ability to love, plan, dream, and create. It would not be reasonable to assume that the creature could be any more perfect than the Creator, since it was from Him that the whole universe came to be, and human existence evolved. If we, as created human beings, exist in the universe, it is only reasonable to expect that the primordial source of the universe, i.e., the Divine, should also possess, in perfection, our same attributes. We can presume that

---

[80] This division originates with Porphyry and Plotinus. Cf. Plotinus, *Enneads* III, pp. 8, 1-10.

consciousness, freedom, and the ability to love are also found in God, but obviously, in a form completely different from ours.

God is a Person. And if this is the case, it is logical to suppose that, among the myriads of galaxies and billions of stars, to Him the most interesting, most important, and most precious entity is the infinitesimal human being with the faculty for at least limited perception and reception of His Being. And therefore, it is indeed reasonable to assume that God would try to approach humankind, manifesting Himself in this world of space and time, so that we may come to apprehend and receive Him.

Once this is recognized, one of the most important tasks for people is to search and find out if such instances have happened in the past—to see whether there are signs of God entering the world and giving signals of Himself, to discover the possible traces He has left in history.

4. The signs of credibility

We Christians believe that all this has really happened. God entered the world, left traces of Himself in the history of humankind, and wants to come into contact with us. He addressed certain individuals (e.g., Abraham), inspired the prophets, and finally, in the fullness of time, showed and presented Himself to the world through a human life (that of Christ). This story contains facts that indicate that it was God Himself who acted in these instances.

We believe that these traces are detectable by all people of good will. The signs and facts that confirm God's action in history are called, in theological parlance, the signs of credibility. I suggest reviewing the most important ones of these.

The first one is the image of God in the Bible: the image of a sole, invisible, personal, and creating God. The peoples of the Ancient East imagined gods as part of the world. Poseidon was the embodiment of the ocean, Zeus was a personification of the sky, and Gaia was synonymous with the Earth. They would relate the story of the origin of the world (cosmogony) in close conjunction with the origins of the gods (theogony). By contrast, the people in the Bible realize that God is different from the world. He is not part of the world. He created the world freely by His autonomous decision. The first sentence of the Bible—"In the beginning, God created the heavens and the earth" (Genesis 1:1)—is without parallel in the literature of the Ancient East. This crystal-clear image of God does not evolve from the high cultures of ancient Egypt or Mesopotamia, nor of India or China, but from the heart of the prophets in the pages of the Bible.

Another such sign is the clear moral awareness emerging in the Bible. As has been mentioned earlier (I/3), the absolute moral laws (You shall not kill! You shall not commit adultery! You shall not steal!) arose out of the encounter with a personal, redeeming God. In other cultures of antiquity, these norms are unknown in this depth and lucidity.

The divine origins of the Bible are also suggested by the prophecies in it. The prophets of the Bible speak about the Messiah, who is to bring salvation to the people and the world. Let me quote a single prophecy here, written approximately 550 years before the birth of Christ:

> He was spurned and avoided by men, a man of suffering, knowing pain, like one from whom you turn your face, spurned, and we held him in no esteem. Yet it was our pain that he bore, our sufferings he endured. We thought of him as stricken, struck down by God and afflicted, but he was pierced for our sins, crushed for our iniquity. He bore the punishment that makes us whole, by his wounds we were healed. We had all gone astray like sheep, all following our own way; but the LORD laid upon him the guilt of us all. Though harshly treated, he submitted and did not open his mouth. Like a lamb led to slaughter or a sheep silent before shearers, he did not open his mouth.
>
> Seized and condemned, he was taken away. Who would have thought any more of his destiny? For he was cut off from the land of the living, struck for the sins of his people. He was given a grave among the wicked, a burial place with evildoers, though he had done no wrong, nor was deceit found in his mouth. But it was the LORD's will to crush him with pain. By making his life as a reparation offering, he shall see his offspring, shall lengthen his days, and the LORD's will shall be accomplished through him. Because of his anguish he shall see the light; because of his knowledge he shall be content. My servant, the just one, shall justify the many, their iniquity he shall bear. Therefore I will give him his portion among the many, and he shall divide the spoils with the mighty, because he surrendered himself to death, was counted among the transgressors, bore the sins of many, and interceded for the transgressor (Isaiah 53:3-12).

Reading these lines is shocking! It is as if the prophet were standing under Jesus's cross. There have been people who were led to the Christianity by this one prophecy alone.[81]

The divine origin of the Bible is demonstrated by Jesus's perfect teaching on love, His miracles, His Cross and Resurrection, as well as

---

[81] An example of this is Israel Zolli, Chief Rabbi of Rome. He was baptized Catholic by Pope Pius XII in 1947. Cf. Cabaud, Judith, *Eugenio Zolli, Prophète d'un monde nouveau* (Paris, 2002).

by the new image of God (belief in the Holy Trinity), which developed as a result of the revelations of Christ. These will be discussed in detail in the chapter on Jesus.

Ultimately, the most important sign is that, while reading the Bible, one feels the power and fire of the living God—a fact that is rather hard to describe in rational terms. When meeting and talking with Christ, we do not meet a dead person or cherish the memory of a great man, but are spoken to, touched and reshaped by the living and resurrected Christ.

5. Is it intolerance to regard a single religion as the repository of ultimate truth?

According to many, placing a particular religion (or view of life) above others is the chief reason for intolerance, arrogance, and imperialism appearing time after time in history. There is no denying that, in the name of religion, a great many wrongs have been done in the course of history. These will also be treated in more detail in Chapter 11. Still, strangely enough, the most horrendous acts of intolerance and violence happened to be committed by forces opposing religion. Greco-Roman culture, prevalent at the time of the birth of Christianity, was seemingly extremely tolerant, easily integrating the deities of new ethnicities into the existing pantheon of gods. However, in practice, it crushed nations with gruesome brutality and murdered Christians on a large scale. Ideologically, Christianity claimed universal and full truth, yet in doing so, it acted with a high degree of tolerance, meekness, and openness. At the time of the French Revolution, in the name of liberty, equality and fraternity, more people were sent to the guillotine in one year than during the hundreds of years of the Inquisition altogether. The purportedly humanistic regimes of the 20th century (namely Nazism and Communism) produced the bloodiest reigns of terror in human history thus far. Is it possible, then, that the main hotbed of intolerance in the world is not religion after all?

If somebody believes that the world and life evolved accidentally, that there is nothing after death, and there are no eternal moral laws—for this is also a kind of belief—while claiming that all ideologies and religions are harmful, except for theirs, does that not amount to a rather intolerant position? Does someone urging that all references to religion be banished from the conduct of public affairs—save their own world view—not speak of an arrogant attitude? Do not those proclaiming that religions are culture-dependent, and therefore no truth value should be attributed to them, make a markedly culture-dependent claim absolutizing their own western, skeptical, nihilistic ideology?

Others say that religion is essentially discriminatory, that it discriminates against non-believers and those who think differently. However, what is really discriminatory is complete *laïcité* and secularism, which excludes much of the Earth's population, people with any religious conviction, from the public square. The point is not supposed to be to ban or silence convictions but to learn to esteem and respect communities with different ways of thinking and let them live.[82]

Christianity does not function as a straitjacket that destroys cultures and individuals. African Christianity is African in character, with dances, old tribal customs, and an African-style theology. In many instances, African languages were rescued and described by Christian missionaries. What tends to strangle religions and devour cultures is, rather, modern, occidental, economic imperialism with its ubiquitously uniform McDonald's restaurants, homogeneous motion pictures, and skeptical western view of the world.

6. Why Christ, and not Buddha or Mohamed?

Our most important reservations about Buddhism were delineated above (IV/9).

In relation to Islam, the following three points—the negation of human reason, the presence of violence, and pedophilia—are outlined as indicative of the religion's unmistakably human character.

A. Allah is the greatest

One of the cornerstones of the religion of Mohamed is the boundless power of God. The muezzin[83] summons the faithful to prayer with the call *Allāhu 'akbar!* (Allah is the greatest!) A human being has no other duty than to prostrate him- or herself before God. The word "Islam" itself means "submission." The whole world must be submitted to an all-powerful God. Whether through eloquent persuasion or by means of violence, the whole of mankind must worship God.

---

[82] Cf. Keller, Timothy, *The Reason for God* (London, 2009), pp. 11-21.
[83] a man who calls Muslims to prayer from the minaret of a mosque.

In general, with regard to divine revelation, human reason and freedom are not assigned any role in Islam.[84] The words of the Quran are believed to be actual dictated words from heavenly tablets. The Quran is held to be the word of God to the letter. There is no room for interpretation or human thinking. There is no need to reconcile it with reason. The will of God must be accepted blindly. A decision made out of free will is not required.

In his Regensburg address, Pope Benedict XVI highlighted precisely these features. True religion cannot be contrary or hostile to reason. Reason cognizes and explores the same reality that true religion explains at a deeper level. Thus, there may never be any contradiction between the two. Religion without reason could easily become fanatical and superstitious. Conversely, reason without the breadth of religion is unable to justify healing humans, as opposed to cloning humans, or building a solar power plant, as opposed to building a nuclear bomb. Reason and faith are interdependent.[85]

In several places, Islamic tradition speaks about Jesus in a tone of respect. However, time and again, it reproaches Him for being weak, arguing that God's cause failed in Him on Earth. Some passages of the Quran expressly deny Jesus's Crucifixion because it is so incompatible with the world view of Islam.[86] A famous Islamic poem exclaims thus: "O Jesus! For Thou gavest the victory to crime."[87] According to the tradition of Islam, on the last day, Allah will take the Cross and crush it.[88] Indeed, Jesus was not a good prophet for a God who is infinite power and expects blind obedience. But He did not come from such a God—one that demands blind obedience. He came from a God Who asks us to respond by loving Him.

Thus, the first difficulty that may be noted in relation to Islam is its imperfect image of God, along with the resultant insufficient appreciation of human freedom and reason.

---

[84] Of course, Islam had its own great philosophers, such as Avicenna (Abū ʿAlī Sīnā) or Averroes (Ibn Rushd), who worked on harmonizing the Quran with reason. These initiatives, however, failed to develop into dominant tendencies within Islam. Shia Islam is considerably more open to the acceptance of the role of reason in explaining the teachings of the religion than the Sunni branch.

[85] In some other places, Pope Benedict XVI also emphasizes that the "parts" in the world (science, culture, economy, etc.) will only fall into place when man acquires a sense of the "whole" again, forming some idea as to the meaning, cause, and objective of human existence, as such. Cf. Pope Benedict XVI, *Caritas in veritate*, pp. 29-31.

[86] Quran, 4:157.

[87] Lammens, Hendri, *Islam. Beliefs and Institutions* (Methuen & Co. Ltd., London, 1929), p. 51.

[88] Alkhalidi, H., *Introducing Islam* (date and place of publication unknown), p. 19.

B. The presence of violence

The second major apparent difficulty is the presence, commandment, and reality of violence from the beginnings of the religion of Islam. This is also described in the verses of the Quran. Mohamed fought many wars and executed many who refused to succumb. The Quran repeatedly calls for the fight against the infidel: "Allah is clear of the idolaters, and so is His Messenger... And when the forbidden months have passed, kill the idolaters wherever you find them... Fight those among the People of the Book who believe not in Allah, nor in the Last Day, nor hold as unlawful what Allah and His Messenger have declared to be unlawful, nor follow the true religion. Fight them!" (Quran 9:3-6, 29) "And kill them wherever you meet them, and drive them out from where they have driven you out; for

persecution is worse than killing... And fight them until there is no persecution and religion is freely professed for Allah" (2:192-194). "And when you meet in regular battle those who disbelieve, smite their necks" (47:5). "So be not slack and seek not for peace; for you will certainly have the upper hand" (47:36; cf. 8:39; 22:78; 66:9). The history of Islam has been intertwined with wars of conquest from the outset.[89]

---

[89] Eliade, Mircea, *A History of Religious Ideas, vol. III* (University of Chicago Press, Chicago, IL, 1985), pp. 64, 66.

These orders in the Quran are read by a number of Muslim thinkers, especially by the adherents of mystical movements, as referring to the victory over the bad in ourselves, as well as to proper thinking and action (*ijtihad*). They regard the calls of the Quran as pertinent to the inner battle to be fought in the context of words, thoughts, and intentions.

Islam's summons to fight is unfortunately related to the presence of violence and is therefore hard to remedy. Nevertheless, we expect and call on the teachers and believers of the religion of Islam to reject all forms of violence against humans and to respect freedom of religion and freedom of conscience.

C. Aisha

Mohamed had eleven wives. According to the tradition of Islam, he had received special permission for this from Allah (Quran 33:50). The last one, Aisha, was seven years old when Mohamed married her.[90] Could any pure divine message come through such a channel?

7. The treasures of Islam

The religion of Islam has countless genuine treasures and values. It believes that God is infinitely powerful, yet at the same time, merciful and gracious (*Rahman*).[91] Following the example of Ibrahim (Abraham), Islamic believers subject themselves to the inscrutable will of God.[92] The basic convictions of Islam include belief in a pure God, who accepts only pure deeds. Whatever one desires for oneself, one also ought to do to one's neighbor. No one should do harm to themselves or others.[93] Every Islamic believer who has the means is obliged to help the poor by giving alms (*zakat*).[94] Islam prohibits taking an oath, the falsification of weights and measures, theft, unchastity and fornication, and prescribes respect for parents and forgiveness.[95]

Islamic mysticism boasts outstanding figures such as al-Hallaj or Maulana Jalaluddin Rumi, who reached similar heights in the love of God and union with Him as Meister Eckhardt or Saint John the Baptist.[96]

---

[90] Sahih al-Bukhari, 7:62-64.
[91] Cf. Quran 1:1.
[92] Cf. Quran, 2:130-131.
[93] Cf. the website of Imam Kamil Mufti: www.islamreligion.com, accessed July 7, 2023.
[94] Cf. Quran, 2:43.
[95] Cf. Quran, 2:224-225; 17:35; 5:38; 7:31; 4:16; 17:23; 42:38-43.
[96] Schimmel, Annmarie, *Mystische Dimensionen des Islam* (Frankfurt am Main, 1995), pp. 100-120, 438-462.

8. Divine grace in other religions

Christians are convinced of the authenticity of biblical revelation because they see the signs that show that it cannot be the product of human effort (cf. V/4). In other religions, such signs are absent, or there are features in conflict with the precepts of reason and the moral good.

Nonetheless, Christianity acknowledges that other religions also possess numerous values, and God's grace works in these religions as well. In a number of instances, a Buddhist, Islamic believer, or Hindu person may lead a significantly more saintly life than a Christian.

One of the most fundamental laws or *weltanschauung*[97] of Hinduism is justice (*dharma*). *Dharma* comprises respect for life and honoring the order and harmony of the world. The love of nature and all living beings, along with a gentle serenity, informing the lives of many Buddhists, is likewise admirable. The lives of many Buddhist monks, spent in meditation, purity, and simplicity could be seen as exemplary. Similarly, the powerful and solid faith of a number of Islamic believers could also be an object of astonishment and envy.

All people of good will, abiding by their conscience, which impels them to do what is right and eschew what is bad—no matter what religion they observe, whether they are in the process of searching for God, or live their lives as skeptics—may find the mystery of God's love and thereby attain eternal salvation (cf. Second Vatican Council, Lumen gentium 16; Gaudium et Spes 22).

9. Does it matter what we believe in?

Many say that what is important is that we should believe in something, and what that something actually is, is beside the point. There is some truth to this. It is undoubtedly important and invigorating to be a believer. They say that the specific theses of particular religions are of the essence from the point of view of faith, and any eventual errors found in individual religions will be corrected by the human heart made by the Creator.[98]

However, it still matters what we believe in. Should someone design their own grab handle and take it with them while traveling on a crowded commuter train and hold onto it? When the train brakes, they will not be restrained by this handle. Perhaps it does matter, after all, whether what we believe in is objectively true or not.

---

[97] a particular philosophy or view of life
[98] This is why Tertullian called the soul Christian by nature *(Apologeticum* 17,6).

10. Take up and read!

Dear Reader,

We have arrived at the proposition that God spoke to humankind. Take the Book of Books in your hand—the book that has and continues to have an amazing impact on the history of humankind. Open this book and start browsing and reading. Allow the living Christ to step out of the Bible's pages and step into your life.

Mohamed – Buddha – and Jesus

According to a parable, a man once fell into a deep hole. Mohamed passed by. He stopped and said to the man, "This is the will of Allah. Accept it." Then Buddha passed by. He saw the man, sat down on the edge of the hole, and started to teach him to meditate upon the fact that suffering was an illusion. Then came Jesus. He saw the man, descended into the hole, carried up the unfortunate man on His shoulders, and treated him to a meal.

Good Friday
by Christina Rosetti

Am I a stone, and not a sheep,
That I can stand, O Christ, beneath Thy cross,
To number drop by drop Thy blood's slow loss,
And yet not weep?
Not so those women loved
Who with exceeding grief lamented Thee;
Not so fallen Peter, weeping bitterly;
Not so the thief was moved;
Not so the sun and moon,
Which hid their faces in a starless sky,
A horror of great darkness at broad noon—
I, only I.
Yet give not o'er,
But seek Thy sheep, true Shepherd of the flock;
Greater than Moses, turn and look once more
And smite this rock.

VI. The Bible Is Too Human and Frail

In the Bible, we sometimes read things that might shake our faith in its divine origins: historical and scientific abnormalities and even manifestations of violence and immorality. Is this book really the Word of God and not the words of fallible men?

1. God spoke through humans

When God wanted to reveal Himself to mankind, He would speak through historical events, in human language, and via human beings. A person is never simply an instrument in God's hands, but His partner. God respects a person's freedom and individuality. Far from destroying these qualities, He elevates them.

Therefore, the Bible is the Word of God, albeit transmitted via human words, human concepts, human culture and events. God's message was filtered through the souls, personalities, and cultures of human authors. This also means that the Bible has absorbed the diverse limitations of these human authors: historical and scientific errors and inaccuracies, as well as even religious and moral imperfections.

2. Historical and scientific imperfections in the Bible

In the story of creation, for example, we read that God created the sky as a canopy to separate the waters below and above it (Genesis 1:6-8). Indeed, antiquity conceived of the sky as a vault. Opening the windows of the heavens would precipitate rain (cf. Genesis 7:11). God did not correct the worldview of the human authors of Genesis. Even through this particular worldview, He was able to communicate His message clearly: He is Creator of all, and He created everything to be good. The Book of Leviticus presents a list of clean and unclean animals. One of the main considerations in this division had to do with the fact that animals that chew the cud were regarded as unclean. It may come as a surprise that the enumeration of ruminants includes the hare (Leviticus 11:6). God does not rectify the gap in the author's zoological knowledge. Despite this fault, He can convey His message perfectly.

In addition, the Bible contains a few historical inaccuracies. For instance, Belshazzar was not the son of Nebuchadnezzar (as Daniel 5:2 suggests), but of Nabonidus. Darius was not the king of the Medes but of the Persians and did not reign before Cyrus but after him (contrary to the claims in Daniel 6:1-29). In antiquity, it was not an easy job to ascertain historical data. In many cases, events were described based on hearsay. Yet God was able to deliver His message notwithstanding these shortcomings.

In saying this, I do not mean to propose that the overall trustworthiness of the Bible does not cover the historical perspective. In most instances, the data in the Bible is accurate. This is frequently supported by a range of archeological finds. For example, the underground aqueduct built by Hezekiah (referenced several times in the Bible) and its inscription have been found. Among the ruins of the city of Tel Lachis, letters written on shards of pottery dating from the time of the 587 siege of Jerusalem, which provide dramatic reports of the same events as those mentioned in the Bible, have been unearthed. Near the walls of Jerusalem, a clay seal was discovered with the text "Baruch, son of Neriah." It was the name of the Prophet Baruch, scribe of Jeremiah, as known from the Bible, that was uncovered by archeologists exploring the ruins of the devastated city. The Bible is a reliable work, even from a historical point of view, though its real value is not derived from this quality, but from the fact that its books were inspired by the power of God.

3. Moral and religious imperfections in the Bible

What presents a devout reader with the greatest difficulty is the moral and religious imperfections of the Bible. For example, the lives of the Patriarchs (Abraham, Isaac and Jacob) were not exemplary in many ways. Abraham denied that Sara was his wife and chose to surrender her so that he could save his own life (Genesis 12:10-20). Jacob deceived his blind father, thereby obtaining his brother's birthright and blessing (Genesis 27). Subsequently, it is repeatedly noted that God commands the people occupying the Promised Land to kill everyone living there, including women and children (Deuteronomy 2:34; 3:6; 20:16-18; Josh. 6:21; 8:24-25).

The Bible is made up of the Old Testament (approximately 80%), with writings spanning 1200-1300 B.C. to about 445 B.C., and the New Testament (approximately 20%), written within about 70 years of Christ's death. Imperfections in the Old Testament do not come from God but from the human authors of the Bible. At that time, many believed that God was only their God, and they were His chosen ones; their enemies were seen as God's enemies, and their wars were thought of as holy wars. Thus, it seemed natural to them that it was

God Himself who ordered them to exterminate their foes. Of course, God never ordered anyone to commit genocide and never will. It goes without saying that all the nations of the world, and every single human being in it, are dear to Him. Mankind, however, was slow to understand God's message. God nurtured people gradually, akin to a father raising his son.[99]

In reviewing the biblical storyline from Abraham to Christ, it becomes apparent that, initially, the divine message mingled with a strong human element, and it would take a long time for God's message to clear up and crystallize. The message became definite and complete only in the revelation of Jesus Christ and the teachings of the New Testament. The interpretation criterion for the preceding parts—the Old Testament books of the Bible, is Christ. The Old Testament is to be read and through the lens of the New Testament. Whatever points to Christ and is in tune with Him is to be regarded as God's message. The Old Testament unfolds the full message of God only when read in the light of Christ's fulfillment. From the outset, the Bible is, by nature, oriented toward Him. Every word of the Bible gains its whole and genuine meaning in Jesus Christ, the living Divine Word, the One in Whom the Word was made flesh (John 1:1).

The Church has encapsulated the perfect morality and teachings of Christ, as given to us through Scripture as well as Church Tradition, in the book, the *Catechism of the Catholic Church*. Would Christ be loving and just if He gave us differing moral truths and abandoned individuals to determine the right answers on their own? No. God, like a good and loving parent, has given the world His divine revelation and made His moral teachings clear so as to bring souls into safety.

The following story happened in Germany: a young girl went to places of entertainment frequently, neglected her studies, was barely in touch with her parents, and finally started to use drugs. The people around her tried to help and warn her in various ways, but to no avail. They succeeded in taking her to a Christian youth community with a priest trained in psychology. The priest even talked with the girl a few times, but these attempts also came to nothing.

In the summer, the girl traveled to Italy to work. When she returned home, it was as if she was a different person. She was kind and cheerful, started to take her studies seriously, gave up her excessive partying, and stopped using drugs. The priest in the community asked her what the reason for this enormous change was. He probably thought it must have been one of their conversations that had triggered something. But the girl replied, "Not at all! In Italy, I started working in a pizzeria. There was a cook who was not nearly as lenient with me as you were. He said to me, one day, 'Hey, you girl! I say there's something wrong with you! You're as sad as three days of rainy

---

[99] Saint John Chrysostom, *On the Incomprehensible Nature of God* I.6 (*PG* 48,707).

82

weather. You're missing something. You should take out the Bible, open it, and let Jesus step forward from its pages and come into your life.' I told him that I didn't believe in things like that. But the idea just stayed with me. One evening a few weeks later, when I was alone, I took out a Bible and started to read it. Then I started reading it more and more frequently. And one night, it did happen! Jesus stepped out from the pages of the Bible and entered my heart."

When I studied in Israel, I met Father Abraham, a Catholic priest of Jewish descent. He was born in Jerusalem. His parents sent him to the Institute of the Brothers of the Christian Schools run by the De La Salle Christian Brothers, owing to the school's high standards, but they made him take a solemn promise not to write a single letter on Saturdays and avoid even looking at the God of the Christians (by the latter, they meant the Cross). One day, the child was given a small edition of the New Testament by a Protestant evangelizer on the street. When he went home, he started reading it. When his father saw that, he completely lost his temper. He snatched the book from the boy's hands, tore it into pieces, and trampled on it. The child wondered with astonishment what that book his parents were so fearful of could possibly be. The young boy would often ask the rabbi when the Messiah was to come and how He could be recognized. The rabbi tended to be evasive and kept saying that it was something of a mystery, which did not need to be talked about so much. The boy was bothered by this constant avoidance of speaking about the most important question.

Then, during World War II, he was taken captive. Over the fence of the POW camp, a woman dropped a copy of the complete Bible for him. This was how, for the second time in his life, Christ's message was handed over to him, as though by Providence. He began to literally devour the New Testament. Within a few days, he came to the realization that whatever the Old Testament prophesied was fulfilled in Christ. Faith was born in his heart. As he said, he felt that the pages and messages of the Old Testament had been black-and-white before, but now they were suddenly filled with colors. He said, "I have been awash with joy ever since!" Some days later, he even decided to become a priest. He went from kibbutz to kibbutz,[100] speaking about Jesus wherever he could, always emphasizing that he was not a converted Jew, but a fulfilled Jew.

---

[100] An intentional community in Israel that was traditionally based on agriculture.

My Mother's Bible
by George P. Morris

This book is all that is left me now!
Tears will unbidden start.
With faltering lip, and throbbing brow,
I press it to my heart.
For many generations passed,
Here is our family tree;
My mother's hands this Bible clasped.
She dying gave it me.

Thou truest friend, man ever knew,
Thy constancy I've tried;
When all were false, I found thee true,
My counselors and guide.
The mines of earth no treasures give,
That could this volume buy;
In teaching me the way to live,
It taught me how to die.

VII. Jesus

Some maintain that nothing certain may be known about Jesus. His character is but the product of legends. Christians began venerating Him as God from the age of Constantine the Great, they say, and at that time, anything contradicting this belief was expunged from the texts of the Gospels. Conversely, others are of the opinion that Jesus was a wise teacher, somebody who, like Socrates or Buddha, deserves attention. Claiming anything more than this would be foolish. Still others assert that Jesus is a living Person, the Savior of the World. In Him and through Him, God revealed Himself and presented Himself to the world.

1. Jesus: a real historical figure?

Sources on Jesus other than Christian ones have also been preserved. The Roman historian Tacitus (ca. AD 115-117), as part of his account of the persecution of Christians under Nero, mentions that Christians were followers of a person called Jesus crucified by Pontius Pilate, Prefect (Governor) of Judea (*The Annals*, *XV*, pp. 44, 2). Suetonius (ca. AD 119) also includes a reference to Christ in one of his historical works (*Vita Neronis XVI*, p. 2; cf. *Vita Claudii, XXV*, p. 4).

Jewish historiographer Josephus Flavius (AD 38-100) alludes to Jesus in several places, as well (*Antiquities of the Jews*, *XVIII*, pp. 63-64; *XX*, p. 200). Although Christian insertions were added to his text subsequently, scholars have been confident in reconstructing Josephus's original text. In the following paragraph from Josephus, the words in parentheses are the insertions of a Christian copyist from a later period. The italicized phrases represent typical features of Josephus's style, and expressions that he favored. "Now there was about this time Jesus, a *wise man*, (if it be lawful to call him a man), for he was a doer of *wonderful works*,[101] teacher of such men as *receive the truth with pleasure*.[102] He *drew over to him many* (He was the Christ). And when *Pilate*, at the suggestion of the principal men amongst us, had condemned him to the cross, those that loved him at the first did not forsake him (for he appeared to them alive again the third day; as the divine prophets had foretold these and ten thousand other wonderful things concerning him). And the *tribe of Christians*,[103] so named from him, are not extinct at this day."[104]

Jewish rabbinic sources contain several allusions to Jesus. They describe Him as someone who deluded the people. In some places, He is called a magician in reference to His miracles (b Sanh 43a).[105]

---

[101] an expression favored by Josephus.
[102] an expression favored by Josephus.
[103] In other places, Josephus speaks of the tribe of the Jews. King Agrippa (in the writing of Josephus) uses the phrase "your tribe."
[104] For highlights of the original writings, cf. Schürer, Emil, *The history of the Jewish people in the age of Jesus Christ I*, ed. G. Vermes, F. Millar, M. Black (Edinburgh, 1973), pp. 428-441.
[105] Ed. Goldschmidt, Lazarus, *Der Babylonische Talmud*, (Frankfurt am Main, 1996) VIII, pp. 631-632.

Archaeological and literary records relating to quite a few of the characters of the Gospel have survived. In Caesarea, an inscription documenting the name of Pilate was identified on a stone slab. In Jerusalem, in the cemetery by the brook Cedron, an ossuary[106] dating

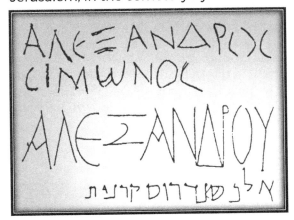

from the time of Christ, was uncovered, displaying the words, "Alexander, Son of Simon of Cyrene." The Gospel reports that, at the time of Jesus's Crucifixion, a man passing by, Simon of Cyrene, father of Alexander and Rufus, was forced to carry Jesus's cross (Mark 15:21). It is almost beyond any doubt that Alexander, whose ossuary archaeologists chanced upon, was one of the sons of this Simon of Cyrene!

Finally, an abundance of historically reliable data on Jesus is supplied by the four Gospels and other early Christian writings. These works were written in the first century AD, a few decades after the events they describe. In conclusion, it seems reasonable to suggest that Jesus is a fairly well-documented character of antiquity, with a large amount of authentic data available regarding His person.

2. Are the Gospels late legends?

The four Gospels were composed shortly after the events of Jesus's life. The Gospel of Mark is the oldest, probably written between AD 64 and 70.[107] According to the testimony of Papias, Bishop of Hierapolis (AD 130) in modern day Pamukkale, Turkey, Mark was the interpreter of Peter the Apostle in Rome. This claim is in harmony with the fact that his Gospel is rich in Latinisms (e.g., *legion, centurion, quadrans*).

Meanwhile, a different collection, the so-called Logia (Logienquelle) containing the sayings and teachings of Jesus was compiled. This work was produced in Northern Palestine, or Syria,

---

[106] a container of bones for burial purposes
[107] Scholars have established the date of composition with reference to the fact that Jesus's prediction of the *destruction of Jerusalem* (70 AD) is described by Mark in blurry *biblical* terms (cf. Daniel 9:27; 11:31; 12:11) as part of a sequence of events constituting the *end of the world* (Mark 13). Matthew and Luke *separate* the account of the destruction of the city from the end of the world and even include *specific details* in the prophecy (cf. Matthew 22:7; Luke 19:43). As pointed out by most biblical scholars, Mark's Gospel was written before the destruction of Jerusalem, whereas the Gospels of Matthew and Luke were composed after it.

prior to AD 70.

Making use of these two earlier works, Matthew and Luke wrote their Gospels between AD 70 and 90 by incorporating their own information and sources. Sentences from the Gospels of Matthew and Luke are quoted by the Didache (ca. AD 90), and by Saint Clement of Rome (94 AD), Saint Ignatius of Antioch (AD 116), and other early Christian treatises.[108]

The Gospel of John was produced around AD 100. The oldest extant New Testament fragment is the Rylands Papyrus (P52), a copy of the Gospel of John from Egypt, written around AD 125.[109] Therefore, it seems that the four Gospels were composed in a period when many eyewitnesses from Jesus's life were still alive.

3. And what about the apocryphal gospels?

Gospels continued to emerge in the subsequent centuries. Most of these are of no historical value. For instance, experts unanimously claim that the so-called Gospel of Judas, dating from ca. AD 160, is unrelated to the historical Judas. Coming from the creation of a singular Egyptian early Christian sect that regarded Judas as a model, it does not contain a single morsel of historically accessible information on Jesus. Throughout, its words and sentences either recombine information extracted from the four Gospels or reflect the peculiar gnostic ideology of the cult (present in other gnostic writings as well).

Similar observations could be made about the other apocryphal gospels. Yet the so-called *Gospel of Thomas* and the *Protoevangelium of James*, which contain authentic traditions associated with Jesus, represent important exceptions. The Gospel of Thomas was written rather early (ca. AD 140), most probably in a Syriac-speaking area (possibly in Edessa).[110] It contains several sayings by Jesus that go back to verifiable historical

---

[108] Schnelle, Udo, *The New Testament Writings* (London, 1998), pp. 222, 243.
[109] Schnelle, Udo., *The New Testament Writings* (London, 1998), pp. 476-477.
[110] Cameron, Rom, "Thomas, The Gospel of," *The Anchor Bible Dictionary* (ed. D. N. Freedman; New York, 1992) VI, p. 536; Erbetta, M., *Gli apocrifi del Nuovo Testamento. Vangeli I/1* (Casale Monferrato, 1982), p. 260.

tradition. Therefore, in terms of historical research on the life and teaching of Jesus, the Gospel of Thomas serves as a significant source. However, as it was drafted by a Christian group closely related to Gnosticism, its text is informed by gnostic notions and interpretations.

The four Gospels were considered normative and canonical by Ancient Christianity as early as the second century. These four Gospels were included in Papias's list (ca. AD 130), the Muratorian Canon (ca. AD 180), and the writings of Saint Irenaeus (ca. AD 180-190). Guided by the Holy Spirit, the Ancient Church assuredly selected the four oldest gospels, historically authentic and free from false teachings, as canonical writings (i.e., constituting parts of the Bible).

4. Have the texts of the Gospels been falsified or censored?

Dan Brown's adventure story, *The Da Vinci Code*, purports to be an academic account, but on many points, draws from false information, alleging that, during the reign of Emperor Constantine the Great (AD 306/324-337), the texts of the Gospels (and of the New Testament Scriptures, in general) were revised, leading to the omission of parts that were in conflict with the belief in Christ's divinity, which was defined at that time.

Like any good deceiver, Dan Brown also employs half-truths to support his thesis. He refers to ancient texts[111] reporting that, in the second half of the third century AD, a Christian teacher by the name of Lucian modified the text of the Bible in Antioch. He also points to the circumstance that, at the time of Emperor Constantine the Great, the Bible was copied in large quantities in Constantinople, often by order and at the expense of the Emperor.

Indeed, as Saint Jerome recounts, the text of the Bible was corrected and amended by a Christian teacher called Lucian in the third century AD. These modifications, however, did not affect its content. Ancient Christians found it disturbing that the style of the

---

[111] Saint Jerome, *De Viris Illustribus* 77; Epistola 106, 2; Comm. in Paralipomenon, Praefatio; Suidae Lexicon, ad vocem Lukianos.

sacred book they used, the Bible, contained very simplistic expressions in many instances, and occasionally even grammatical errors and poorly constructed sentences. The goal of Lucian (provided Jerome's claim regarding him is trustworthy) and of his associates was to produce a linguistically more elegant Greek biblical text. This version of the Bible did, in fact, reach Constantinople (since many of the Patriarchs of Constantinople moved to the capital from Antioch and would bring their own Antiochian Bibles with them).[112] Thus, these are the minute modicums of truth in the claims advanced in *The Da Vinci Code*. At the same time, Dan Brown cunningly conceals these most important facts:

1. Emendations to the text of the Bible were not ordered and supervised by the Emperor, but part of an internal ecclesiastical process.
2. The text was improved exclusively on grammatical grounds, without any changes to content.
3. Even more importantly, it is a verifiable fact that the pre-Constantinian biblical text (i.e., the one pre-dating the modifications by Lucian) is available in its entirety! The Greek New Testament papyri surviving from the first three centuries completely cover the text of the New Testament. In many cases the fragments of papyri, when put together, one over the other, would cover several times in several layers, parts of the text of the New Testament. There are many parts of texts of the New Testament which are preserved in several papyri (dating from the first three centuries), not just one. In addition, the Latin of the New Testament (*Vetus Latina* and *Vetus Syra*) has also been preserved. Both translations date to ca. AD 200, thus bearing testimony to the condition of the text of the New Testament around AD 200. Essentially, these translations are also in full agreement with the texts recovered from the surviving Greek papyri.[113]

In other words, reconstructing the original text of the New Testament (including the Gospels) and seeking to determine what might have been subsequently left out of it, in no way leads to cracking a scientific mystery. Nothing was left out. The text of the New Testament is the most verified text of antiquity, with the largest number of written records and testimonies: approximately 90 papyri,

---

[112] Aland, Kurt; Aland, Barbara, *Der Text des Neuen Testaments* (Stuttgart, 1982), pp. 74-75.

[113] Aland, Kurt; Aland, Barbara, *Der Text des Neuen Testaments* (Stuttgart, 1982), pp. 192-196; 199-202. Vetus Syra is a term denoting the Syriac text published by Cuerton and found in the codices discovered in Saint Catherine's Monastery in Sinai (i.e.„pre-dating the Peshitta). Cf. Böhlig, A., "Bibelübersetzungen," *Bibel- Lexikon* (ed. H. Haag; Leipzig, 1969), pp. 232-234; Thiele, W., "Vetus Latina," *Bibel-Lexikon* (ed. H. Haag; Leipzig, 1969), pp. 1846-1848.

274 majuscule-script codices (written entirely in capital letters), 2795 minuscule-script codices (written entirely in lower case letters), and 2207 lectionaries (collections of readings). The oldest and most authentic written records—P75 (the Bodmer Papyri), B (Codex Vaticanus), א (Codex Sinaiticus), C (Codex Ephraemi), 33 (Paris, "the queen of minuscules"), and bo sa (Coptic translations)—contain the genuine text of the New Testament, devoid of any subsequent distortions. Contemporary academic text versions[114] contain this

biblical text (pre-dating the modifications by Lucian), and modern translations of the Bible also rely on it as their source.[115] The original text may easily be compared to the text of the so-called Byzantine text-type going back to Lucian—the only evident differences being minor stylistic changes.

5. Do the Gospels contain historically reliable data on Jesus?

Many say that the events described in the Gospels are legends, and as such, are historically unreliable. One can infer from the Gospel events only what the first Christians believed about Jesus, not the actual historical Jesus, because they contain information distorted by the zeal of faith.

Countering that claim, it is important to be aware of the following facts. The Gospels were written at a time when many eyewitnesses were still alive. They cannot be the records of made-up legends. The

[114] Nestle, Eberhard; Aland, Kurt, *Novum Testamentum Graece* (Stuttgart, 1993); *The Greek New Testament*, ed. K. Aland - M. Black - C. M. Martini - B. M. Metzger - A. Wikgren (Stuttgart, 1993).

[115] At the time of the Reformation, it was not yet clear which manuscripts contained the text of the Bible in the most authentic form. Erasmus of Rotterdam took the late codices of the so-called Byzantine text-type as a starting point, and, subsequently, Luther and the translators of the King James Bible (KJV) also based their translations on it. Interestingly, it was often the case that the Latin biblical text (dating from AD 200) used by the Catholic Church was closer to the original than the late Greek text utilized by Luther (or the translators of the KJV) since, for the New Testament, the text of the Vulgate used by the Catholic Church adopted the text of the earlier Latin translation (Vetus Latina) produced around AD 200, precisely following the original Greek text. A well-known illustration of this is a line from the story of the nativity of Jesus: "good will toward men" (KJV)—instead of the original phrase, which may seem hard to interpret: "to the people of good will" (i.e., to those who are the recipients of the good will of God, those who are favored and blessed by God).

Apostles—with one exception—all gave their lives for their faith in Christ. Nobody is likely to sacrifice their life for a fairytale invented by themselves. It is hard to imagine how messages contrived out of lies and fantasies could produce such an impact, and how these could be felt to be credible by so many.

With the help of the methods of historical criticism, it is possible to extract from the text of the Gospel those details, events, and words that, in all probability, did happen or were, in fact, spoken. What follows is a brief overview of the criteria of historicity.[116]

1. **Multiple Attestation:** The more sources independent of one another (the Gospel of Mark, the Q Source, i.e., the Logia, Matthew's own traditions, Luke's own traditions, the Gospel of John, the Gospel of Thomas) attest to a particular piece of data on Jesus, the more likely it is authentic.[117]

2. **Dissimilarity:** The more a particular teaching or act traditionally attributed to Jesus differs from the corresponding contemporary Jewish conception and idiom of the Apostolic Church, the more likely the respective tradition is a historically authentic one.
   The Gospels relate a large number of events and sayings by Jesus that were difficult for the first Christian community to understand and accept (e.g., the baptism of Jesus by John the Baptist; Jesus's fear of death and prayer in the Garden of Gethsemane; the shameful flight of the Apostles). Obviously, these are not invented episodes.

3. **Coherence:** If a particular teaching or act of Jesus under scrutiny resembles the deeds and words by Jesus already recognized as authentic, it is safe to conclude that it must be genuine.

4. **Environment:** The more a particular teaching or act traditionally attributed to Jesus fits the characteristic settings of Jesus's public ministry (e.g., no allusions to the delay of the *parousia* or the destruction of Jerusalem), the more likely the tradition concerned is authentic.

5. **Aramaisms:** The easier it is to translate sentences of the Greek Gospels expressing Jesus's teaching into Aramaic (the mother tongue of Jesus), the more likely the tradition they are associated with is historically reliable.

Thus, with the aid of the instruments of historical inquiry, it is possible to highlight a good number of sayings and acts by Jesus that could prompt a critical historian engaging in objective analysis to declare that the respective events were real, and the cited words were

---

[116] Meier, John P., *A Marginal Jew: Rethinking the Historical Jesus* (New York, 1991), pp. 168-201.
[117] Manson, Thomas Walter, *The Teaching of Jesus* (Cambridge, 1935).

indeed uttered by Jesus. An excellent overview of such historical research, as well as of the concomitant research findings, is offered by John P. Meier.[118]

6. Was Jesus only a wise teacher?

Many reach the point of acknowledging the greatness of Jesus. However, all they suggest is that Jesus was only an outstanding person and a wise teacher. This option is not available to us, though, as it can be established historically that Jesus did not deem Himself to be only a wise teacher. Quite the contrary, He acted and spoke as God, as the Son of the Father. The alternative propositions may be formulated along the following lines: He was a fool, or He was a liar and a wicked person (since He knew that He was not a divine being, yet He claimed to be one), or what He says is true, and He was, indeed, more than a great man. There are no more options. It would make no sense to conclude that He was a great man and a wise teacher.[119]

Jesus taught with enormous authority. The great founders of religions always referred to something or someone. Buddha said that he had experienced a major enlightenment and intended to deliver the resulting message to others. Mohamed claimed that he had seen the Angel Gabriel in a vision, entrusting messages to him. The prophets of the Old Testament said that they had been called by the Lord and conveyed His word. Jesus did not refer to anybody or anything. He said, "You have heard that it was said to those of your ancestors, 'You shall not kill.' (To put it differently: *You know that God told your fathers on Mount Sinai, "You shall not kill."*) But I say to you..." (i.e., *I will tell you something more, something better*; Matthew 5:21). Jesus forgave sins (Mark 2:6). Jesus was not just another prophet; He did not proclaim what the old prophets had, encouraging the people to be patient and to expect the coming fulfillment. Jesus said, "This is the time of fulfillment. The Kingdom of God is at hand." (Mark 1:15) When He was asked, "Are you the one who is to come, or should we look for another?" Jesus replied, "Go and tell John what you have seen and heard: the blind regain their sight, the lame walk, lepers are cleansed, the deaf hear, the dead are raised, the poor have the good news proclaimed to them. And blessed is the one who takes no offense at me." (Luke 7:19-23) In other words, the long wait of history is over. I am the One people have been expecting for centuries.

Jesus performed miracles openly and publicly, a fact that His mortal enemies never denied, either. This is part of the reason why they devised the circumspect explanation that He colluded with the chief of the

[118] Meier, John P., *A Marginal Jew* I-IV. (New York, 1991-2009).
[119] Cf. Lewis, C.S., *Mere Christianity* (London, 1952), pp. 28-30; Kreeft, Peter J.; Tacelli, R. K., *Handbook of Catholic Apologetics* (San Francisco, 1994), pp. 166-167.

demons (called "Beelzebub") and received power from him to drive out demons (Mark 3:22). They did not even try to call His healings into question, as these events were seen and experienced by them and the crowd alike. The Jewish historian, Josephus Flavius, around AD 93-94, also noted as a fact, that Jesus performed inexplicable deeds (*Antiquities of the Jews XVIII*, p. 63). Similar evidence is found in the unsympathetic allusions to Jesus in the Talmud.

Of course, should somebody start out from the preconception that miracles are impossible, they will consider such unequivocal reports untrue. The fact that recoveries that cannot be scientifically accounted for happen these days, too, is exemplified, among other things, by the pilgrimage site of Lourdes. A committee consisting of mainly atheist physicians diagnose every patient arriving there who is willing to take the test. Anyone claiming to have been healed at the pilgrimage site is given a second diagnosis after dipping into the miraculous spring water baths there, and the two diagnoses are subsequently juxtaposed. Year after year, the committee of doctors concludes that scientifically unexplainable events have taken place. Could it then be the case that the wrong preconceptions of some are the reason for the report of inexplicable healings, and not the historically verifiable facts?

Jesus said that those who listen to His words and live their lives accordingly, build the house of their lives on a rock. However, whoever fails to live according to His teaching will see the house of their life collapse (Matt. 7:24-27). Jesus taught that everyone who acknowledges Him before others, He will also acknowledge before the throne of God. Conversely, whoever is ashamed of Him in this earthly life, He will be ashamed of on the final day (Mark 8:38). The ultimate fate of every human being will depend on whether he or she decides for Jesus.

Jesus not only taught that we should love God and follow God. What he taught was "Follow Me!" (Mark 1:17) He said, "Whoever loves father or mother more than me is not worthy of me, and whoever loves son or daughter more than me is not worthy of me." (Matthew 10:37)

Who is this man who speaks like this? More and more people around Jesus would raise this question. The disciples asked, "Who then is this whom even wind and sea obey?" (Mark 4:41) His opponents inquired, "Who do you make yourself out to be?" (John 8:53) Among the people around Jesus, the question of who He was, increasingly became the focus of attention. Jesus Himself also asked His disciples, "But who do you say that I am?" Peter said to him in reply, "You are the Messiah." (Mark 8:29)

Jesus did not address God with the words "My God,"[120] but called Him "Abba" (i.e., "Father"; Mark 14:36; Luke 11:2). He spoke about the Temple as the house of His Father: a place where He was at home and had full power (cf. John 2:16).

Upon His entry into Jerusalem, Jesus deliberately fulfilled the old prophecies. He entered the city riding a donkey and expelled the merchants from the Temple, as Zechariah foretold (Zechariah 9:9; 14:21). The people also recognized the signs and greeted Him as the Messiah: "Hosanna! Blessed is he who comes in the name of the Lord! Blessed is the kingdom of our father David that is to come!" (Mark 11:9-10)

Jesus related the Passover Supper, the most sacred ritual of the Jews, to Himself. He said that the old deliverance was but a shadow of the real one, which was to come now through His broken body and death. In Him a new and everlasting covenant was being made, one that was only foreshadowed by the first covenant (cf. Mark 14:22-24).

In the charge brought against Him, Jesus was questioned by Caiaphas: "Are you the Messiah, the Son of the Blessed One (i.e., God)?" (Mark 14:61) Jesus knew that if He answered this question in the affirmative, He would be killed. Jesus put His life on the line with His answer and said, "I am; and 'you will see the Son of Man seated at the right hand of the Power (i.e., God) and coming with the clouds of heaven.'" (Mark 14:62)

Jesus did not speak and act like a great man. His words and deeds went well beyond the limits of human existence.

7. Life appeared! (1 John 1:2)

The identity of Jesus as the Messiah and Son of God was confirmed by His Resurrection. In relation to the resurrection of Jesus, three circumstances are worth remembering:

1. The disciples had not anticipated Jesus's Resurrection. Some went home, as if to forget everything as soon as they could (Luke 24:13-24), while others returned to their profession (John 21:3). They were by no means in a heightened state of suspense.

2. Neither Jewry nor Hellenism had any idea about a specific historical figure dying and rising from the dead. The Jews (more precisely, the Pharisees) expected the resurrection of the dead to take place at the end of the history of the world. Those representing Greek thought derided Paul when he spoke of Jesus's Resurrection, saying, "We should like to hear you on this

---

[120] The only exception in this regard are His words spoken on the Cross ("My God, my God, why have you forsaken me"; Mark 15:34), quoting a verse from an Old Testament psalm.

some other time" (Acts 17:32). Thus, it becomes clear that the apostles were not guided by their worldview; they hadn't interpreted an inner spiritual experience as Jesus's Resurrection. On the contrary, they were faced with a fact that compelled them to radically transform their worldview.

3. Finally, a few days after the death of Jesus, the apostles were in the perilous city of Jerusalem again and would soon begin proclaiming that Jesus lives, they have met Him, and He is the Lord and the Messiah. From this point on, their lives would be solely devoted to going around the world happily preaching Christ—all but one ultimately giving their lives for Him.

Between the two events—Jesus's death and the good news of Easter—something had to happen. The very moment of the Resurrection is not described in the Bible because the disciples were not witness to it. However, accounts of their encounters with the Resurrected One are included in the Bible.

These encounters are special. The apostles did not recognize Jesus by His face but by a word or gesture of His (Luke 24:30-31; John 20:16). They were behind closed doors; all of a sudden, Jesus was among them and then He disappeared from before their eyes just as quickly (John 20:19). The descriptions indicate that the apostles experienced something that can hardly be expressed in human words. These encounters regenerated the faith of the apostles, and such an encounter transformed Saul, a persecutor of Christians, into an ardent follower of Jesus (Acts 9:1-19; Galatians 1:11-16).

In Christ, the indestructible life of God appeared in this transient earthly world. This is what the apostles experienced. Humankind gained the ultimate confirmation of eternal life, which it had always hoped for.[121] In Christ, the mystery of God, the mystery of the Creator, and the mystery of the world was revealed. We received the ultimate assurance that God is love, and that every person is, indeed, infinitely important to Him. He came into our world to speak to us in human words, to love with a human heart, and to give Himself fully to us.

---

[121] Eternal life is discussed in more detail in Chapter 12.

8. If He has risen in me, is the Gospel true then?

The famous Lutheran biblical scholar Rudolf Bultmann claimed that
it cannot be ascertained whether Jesus rose from the dead or not, or
whether He did miracles or not. However, he does not see this as a
problem. Faith must be absolute and cannot be based on incidental
historical evidence. He argues that if the Good News of the Gospel
reaches me here and now, and I respond to it with faith, then Christ is
resurrected in me, the Gospel is true and it works.

This is a rather odd point of view. If I cannot know for sure whether
Christ existed, performed miracles, and rose from the dead,
objectively and independently of me—if I cannot be sure that He will
also fulfill my life after my death, why do I think that He could help
me now? Bultmann's system is essentially one of self-salvation. Man
redeems himself through his own act of faith, while the external,
objective reality of redemption (*"extra nos"*) completely disappears.

9. Did faith blur the disciples' vision?

Some say that the faith and enthusiasm of the disciples made it
impossible for them to view Jesus and the events of His life without
bias.

Faith, personal openness, and commitment, however, do not
hinder proper and insightful discoveries. On the contrary, intimate

familiarity can only be attained through faith and commitment. If a scientist begins examining a beautiful bouquet of flowers objectively, detached from emotions, tearing off its petals and analyzing its chemical composition, he or she will never be able to appreciate the beauty and the reality of the bouquet in its profundity. Such an understanding would require a sense of marveling, admiration, and openness. Cool, distant objectivity is not enough when becoming truly acquainted with a person. Love, commitment, and trust are also needed. Reality has layers that are accessible only through faith, openness, trust, and love.

This kind of vision through faith is in no contradiction with scientific truths. Faith probes in the same direction as science. The only difference is that faith employs a different method, and thus, it can delve deeper.

The disciples looked upon Jesus with faith, amazement, and admiration, and it was precisely this that opened their eyes so that they could come to appreciate and accept His full reality.

10. The mystery of salvation

This book does not seek to present or enable access to the entire teaching of Christianity. Nor is it possible to discuss here the reality of salvation at length. Nonetheless, I would like to briefly highlight the core of this teaching.

Many argue that it is a rather barbaric and unbelievable teaching that God forgives the sins of humans at a cost that involves demanding the bloody sacrifice of another being, Christ, in their stead.[122] What kind of god is it that wants to see the blood of his own son, first, so that he can forgive? In what way could the horrible suffering of another living being secure the forgiveness of my sins, and how could it repair the disorderliness and scars that I have caused?

Sin does not consist in people offending God, and as a result, God becoming enraged with people and closing the gates of heaven before them in His wrath. Conversely, salvation does not consist in people propitiating God. In fact, sin consists in people distorting and wounding themselves, their fellow human beings, and the world. Salvation is not an act of humankind to appease God, but an act of God, whereby He comes into this world, so injured by sin, and pours His purifying and recreating love to heal the wounds caused by sin.

---

[122] "This is just as widespread as it is false." Ratzinger, Joseph, *Foi chrétienne hier et aujourd'hui* (Paris, 1976), p. 197. "Reality is considerably simpler. The Son of God came to His own, but they refused to receive Him. He did not come to Earth to have Himself crucified. However, He was able to enter into the midst of the wicked unarmed..." Delumeau, Jean, *Le ragioni di un credente* (Torino, 1987), p. 61. Christ's passion and death were the work of evil. Still, it was turned to our salvation because, notwithstanding all the sins and suffering, He loved until the end and gave up His life out of love.

Paul the Apostle puts it this way: "God was reconciling the world to himself in Christ" (2 Corinthians 5:19). Thus, it was not people who brought reconciliation with God, but it was God who brought reconciliation with the world. The work of redemption does not start out from a furious God who needed to be placated, but from a God whose love is infinite: "For God so loved the world, that he gave his only Son, so that everyone who believes in him might not perish but might have eternal life" (John 3:16).

Sin is not merely a fault in the history of humanity. People were created human by an upward lifting gravitational Force and meant for relationship with God. This link is in the heart of our humanity. If it is injured or weakened, humankind, as a whole, is hurt. There would be nothing that could elevate people above their selfishness, no upward lifting Force, that mysterious Third (cf. Endre Gyökössy), who would raise married couples above their grievances and limitations, nor any Force that could hold a society together and make it human and livable. Sin is a blow to humanity that causes people to become ill in their very essence. Therefore, salvation is a matter of life or death for humans.

Why did then the terrible suffering of the Cross of Jesus become part of the work of salvation? God came into this world that is distorted by sin, a sordid world that expelled and destroyed the innocent and the pure (cf. John 1:3,11). God's forgiveness was not simply a merciful gesture saying, "I am not angry." His forgiveness also meant that He entered our sin-ravaged world, became one with us, and permeated our existence with His love, so as to restore the world and us to the order of God's love.[123]

It is true, even of human love, that if someone loves another person, they will also shoulder that person's pain, burdens, and wounds, healing and recreating him or her with their love.

The Cross of Jesus shouts into the world to the end of history that God's love for us transcends death. We are infinitely important to God: God entered into the inferno of our sins and poured out the stream of His blood and His healing love upon us (cf. John 19:34-35; Zechariah 12:10-13:1). With His arms extended on the Cross, He embraced us and drew us to Himself (cf. John 12:32). Life has appeared on Earth again so that we might live again; love has appeared and has been poured out so that we might love again (cf. Romans 5:5).

---

[123] Cf. Ratzinger, Joseph, Pope Benedict XVI, *Jesus of Nazareth: Holy Week* (Ignatius Press, San Francisco, 2011), pp. 230-232. Ratzinger, Joseph, *Dogma und Verkündigung* (Munich, 1977), p. 334; Nichols, Aidan, *La pensée de Benoît XVI* (Geneva, 2008), p. 158.

11. God is love

The world is breathtakingly beautiful. Anyone regarding it with an open heart may derive the sensation from it that the Creator, out of Whom all this has arisen, is the ultimate Beauty and Goodness, and the Source of all beauty and goodness.

The Prophet Isaiah wrote the following:

> You shall be a glorious crown in the hand of the LORD, a royal diadem in the hand of your God. No more shall you be called "Forsaken," nor your land called "Desolate," but you shall be called "My Delight is in her," and your land "Espoused." For the LORD delights in you, and your land shall be espoused. For as a young man marries a virgin, your Builder shall marry you; and as a bridegroom rejoices in his bride, so shall your God rejoice in you. (Isaiah 62:3-5)

As a king puts on his crown and proudly walks out to appear before his subjects—says the prophet—so does our God feel about us. God's crown and pride is humankind. As a bridegroom can rejoice over the bride, so does our God rejoice over us. God's joy is humanity. He loves us more than the best parent may love their child, the best grandparent may love their grandchild, or the best spouse may love their partner.

God's love was ultimately and radically revealed by the Cross of Jesus. Paul the Apostle exclaimed, "God...has loved me and given himself up for me." (Galatians 2:20)

Dear Reader,

God's infinite goodness is also poured on you! He would like to make your life complete (John 10:10). Can you open the door of your life so that His light may shine upon you?

12. The Holy Trinity

Christianity is a monotheistic religion. The ultimate source of the diversity of the world is the Fullness of Being: the Only God. However, the unity of God is not a monolithic one. In God, there is life.

It is through the teachings and actions of Jesus Christ that God revealed Himself as the Holy Trinity: Three Divine Persons, so completely self-giving in their eternal love for one another that they are One. This attribute of God first became known when God the Father sent His only Son, Jesus Christ, the Second Person of the Trinity, to Earth: the eternal "Word became flesh and made his dwelling among us" (John 1:14). Then Jesus made it clear to His disciples that He was not just fully human, but fully God: "The Father and I are one" (John 10:30). Before leaving his disciples to return to the Father, Jesus promised that He would send them the Advocate, the Holy Spirit, Who is also God: "The Advocate, the holy Spirit that the Father will send in my name—he will teach you everything and remind you of all that [I] told you" (John 14:26). He also told them: "And I will ask the Father, and he will give you another Advocate to be with you always, the Spirit of truth, which the world cannot accept, because it neither sees nor knows it. But you know it, because it remains with you, and will be in you." (John 14:16-17) Jesus was, of course, true to His promise. After the Resurrection, He breathed on His disciples and said to them, "Receive the holy Spirit" (John 14:22). This filled them with such great love, joy, power, courage, and spiritual gifts, transforming them from sad, scared, persecuted followers, that they went on to proclaim Jesus's Name boldly, even unto death. Thus, Jesus Christ revealed, step by step, God's nature of Three Divine Persons in One.

Through Christ, this living God was revealed to us. God revealed Himself as One Who is a Father, as One Who has a Son, as One Who sends His Spirit. Life springs from Him, never-ending procreation and regeneration. The Father is called Father because He possesses the fullness of divinity by giving it. He begets the Son from all eternity and keeps nothing for Himself but delivers everything to the Son. The Son is called Son because He is begotten from all eternity. He possesses the fullness of divinity by receiving it, keeping nothing for Himself but returning everything to the Father immediately. Finally, the Holy Spirit is the Fullness of Being and the Love emanating from the Two. Together the Three share a constant ecstasy of love, for God is Love.

The world is the trace and image of this Triune God—from the dance of nuclei and electrons to the love between man and woman. We were born to enter this flow of divine love, to share in this divine dance, and to learn the Holy Trinity's melody of love.

Once, a simple workman became a convert. His fellow workers would often mock him badly for it. One day, one of them began asking him, "What do you know about Jesus that makes you believe in Him so much? Do you know which cities He taught in, how many parables He told, or what philosophers built upon His teachings?"

The man could not answer a single question. In the end he said, "I am ashamed that I know so little about Jesus. But, after all, I do know something about Him. Before I learned about Him, I was a heavy drinker and an unhappy man. I caused an awful lot of pain and suffering to my wife, and my children would hide from me whenever they saw me. Since I've gotten to know Jesus, I have stopped drinking, my wife and I have been living in love and harmony, and these days, my children run toward me and give me hugs when I get home. This is what Jesus has done for me. This is what I know about Him."

The following is from a personal letter written by the famous Russian novelist Fyodor Dostoevsky (1821-1881):

"I want to say to you about myself, that I am a child of this age, a child of unfaith and skepticism, and probably (indeed I know it) shall remain so to the end of my life. How dreadfully has it tormented me (and torments me even now)—this longing for faith, which is all the stronger for the proofs I have against it. And yet God gives me sometimes moments of perfect peace; in such moments I love and believe that I am loved; in such moments I have formulated my creed,[124] wherein all is clear and holy to me. This creed is extremely simple; here it is: I believe there is nothing lovelier, deeper, and more sympathetic, more rational, more manly, and more perfect than the Savior; I say to myself with jealous love that not only is there no one else like Him, but that there could be no one. I would even say more: If anyone could prove to me that Christ is outside the truth, and if the truth really did exclude Christ, I should prefer to stay with Christ and not with the truth." (Dostoevsky's letter to Mme. N. D. Fonvisin)[125]

---

[124] In the original, this word literally means 'symbol of faith', corresponding to Early Christian terminology.
[125] Cf. Colburn Mayne, E., *Letters of Fyodor Michaiiovitch Dostoevsky to his Family and Friends* (London, Chatto & Windus, 1914), pp. 67-68.

Christ by Jenő Dsida

My Christ,
I will take Your picture off my wall.
I feel its lines and colors a folly;
never could I imagine You as You are here:
with such shining blue eyes,
so content and serene,
with such a bright face,
of so soft a light red,
like a rose dropped in milk.

I have seen You many a night,
I have heard You,
and I know that You are simple and humble,
that You were poor, gray, weary,
and akin to us.

Sleeplessly, you wandered the road,
the path of the outcast,
the vales of hunger,
and on the horizon of Your tormenting concerns,
the flames of Your crumbling Jerusalem
licked the sky.

Your voice stirred painful waves when,
after much speaking, hoarse again,
You began to talk.
Your torn and faded garment
was thick with the dust of Your long journey.

Your lean face was tanned by wind and sun,
the bronze-red of jaundice,
and from Your two smoldering eyes
onto Your shaggy beard
dropped the tears of God.

VIII. Yes to Jesus – No to the Church?

Perhaps many people get as far as acknowledging Jesus's greatness, and some sort of faith in Him is even born in their hearts. However, they insist that they have no need of the Church, arguing it is repulsive, institutionalized, burdened with sins, and narrow-minded. Yes to Jesus—No to the Church.

1. Jesus's intention

Those thinking in the way described above must come to terms with the disturbing reality that the Church was founded because Jesus wanted it.

Jesus chose twelve disciples (Mark 3:13-19). In doing so, He intended to show that He wished to restore and re-found the People of God, once composed of twelve tribes and built upon the twelve sons of Jacob. Thereby, He created the New People of the New Testament. He entrusted His teaching to His disciples: "The one who listens to you listens to me. Whoever rejects you rejects me" (Luke 10:16). He commended the communication of the forgiveness of sins and the distribution of the fruits of salvation to them: "As the Father has sent me, so I send you." And when he had said this, he breathed on them and said to them, "Receive the holy Spirit. Whose sins you forgive are forgiven them, and whose sins you retain are retained." (John 20:21-22) He entrusted Peter with the responsibility of acting as a shepherd and leader of His flock (Luke 22:31-32; John 21:15-17; Matthew 16:16-19). He enjoined His disciples to proclaim His teaching to all peoples and baptize the nations (Matthew 28:18-20). Jesus had a people and a community of His own. A churchless Jesus is unhistorical.

Jesus promised that He would remain with His Church (Matthew 28:20). He promised that even the gates of hell would not prevail against His Church (Matthew 16:18). He also promised that the Holy Spirit would guide His disciples into all truth and teach them everything (John 14:26; 16:13).

At the Last Supper, He prayed so that His disciples might all be one and that the world might believe that He was sent by the Father (John 17:21). The Church is the sign and the epitome of the sacredness of the union of the human being and God, as well as of the unity of the whole human race (LG 1). The foundation of new churches and congregations is against Jesus's will since acts of that kind shatter precisely this union, inherent in the Church.

2. Humans are essentially social beings

Why is it important to experience faith in community? Why did Christ want the Church? Humans are essentially social beings.[126] We receive life through the union of our birth parents. According to a formulation of the philosophical school of personalism, one may become "I" only in relation to "you." It is in the reflection of another person that we discover ourselves. As babies, we learn to smile from our mother, father, or caregiver smiling at us. Similarly, we learn to speak from being spoken to. We learn to love when our love is accepted by others. We develop self-confidence when others have confidence in us. We become ourselves in engagement with each other. Personal relationships pertain to the very essence of being human.

Humans acquire everything valuable by means of social and

---

[126] Cf. Second Vatican Council, Gaudium et spes 24-25.

historical transmission. From previous generations we receive the language in which our minds think. Knowledge, culture, and art are likewise handed down to us via social transmission. It is only natural that the values of religion are also preserved and transmitted communally by humanity. The grace and presence of God became incarnate into history. Moses already knew what Abraham had experienced because he heard it from the accounts of his ancestors. The Prophet Isaiah, in turn, knew what Abraham and Moses had experienced because he acquired that knowledge from the sacred tradition of his people.

3. The Bible was composed and discovered by the Church

When God spoke to humans, He did not drop a book from the sky— He primarily addressed individuals. He wrote His message on their hearts. The Church, the Old- and New-Testament People of God, predates the Bible.

The books of the Bible featured no sign saying, "Attention! This book is part of the Bible. Please treat it as such." Books not included in the Bible (e.g., the Book of Enoch or 2 Esdras) bore no inscription saying, "Caution! Not part of the Bible. Please do not add it as such." Which books should constitute the Bible was determined and discovered by the Catholic Church, under the guidance of the Holy Spirit.

Christianity adopted the original Old Testament canon[127] of the Jews (the Hebrew Bible), as evidenced by the *Septuagint*. The Septuagint (often abbreviated as LXX) is a translation produced by Jewish scholars in Egypt in the 3rd and 2nd centuries BC. It is the earliest extant Greek translation of the Old Testament from the original Hebrew. The text is evidence of the long Old Testament canon (altogether 46 books with the concluding prophetic books, which anticipate the coming of the Messiah). This canon includes Old Testament books from its latest period, connecting the Old Testament to its fulfillment in Christ in terms of time and content alike.[128]

Subsequently (ca. AD 90), the Jews narrowed down their canon at the Council of Jamnia held in Israel, late in the 1st century AD, in response to Christianity. It was then that Judaism finally declared itself as completely distinct from Christianity (issuing an anathema against the "Nazarenes"), and rejected the Gospels, along with books of the Old Testament that were composed in later times (e.g., Sirach;

---

[127] A biblical canon is a set of texts (also called "books") which a particular Jewish or Christian religious community regards as part of the Bible.
[128] For instance, themes such as the importance of good deeds (Book of Tobit) and faith in eternal life (2 Maccabees; Book of Wisdom) emerge in them.

cf. Mishnah Yadayim[129] 2:13).

Therefore, it may be seen as particularly problematic that Martin Luther (1483-1546), the catalyst and seminal figure of the 16th century Protestant Reformation, chose[130] the short Jewish canon at the Leipzig Debate (1519).[131] This short Jewish canon happened to be specified in a period of Judaism influenced by rather anti-Christian sentiments.

As for the composition of the short canon, contrary to a widespread misconception, it was not defined by the inclusion of only the books written in Hebrew. Several of the deuterocanonical[132] books of the long (ancient) canon were, in fact, in Hebrew. However, because in later periods the Jews did not regard these as sacred books, they stopped copying these scrolls (and occasionally would even destroy them), most of their texts in Hebrew have not survived. Still, in some cases, they have been preserved. Most of Sirach, for example, was found in the Cairo Geniza[133] and at the excavations of Masada.[134]

It must be noted that the authority of the long canon was so great that the deuterocanonical books were appended to editions of the Old Testament for hundreds of years until the 1827 decision of the United Bible Societies to do otherwise. Nowadays, this practice of adding the deuterocanonical books is being reintroduced in many Protestant editions of the Bible (called the ecumenical editions).

The canon of the New Testament was recognized and determined by the Christian community. In response to the heresy of Marcion of Sinope, who deemed only the Gospel of Luke and ten Pauline epistles to be canonical, the canon of the New Testament was affirmed in the second century. One of the most significant and most ancient testimonies in this regard is the Muratorian Canon, recorded in Rome around AD 180.

As even this brief overview clearly demonstrates, the books of the Bible were recognized by the Church. Somebody who does not believe in the Church and does not believe that the Church was and is guided by the Holy Spirit cannot really answer the question as to

[129] The Mishnah or the Mishna is the first major written collection of the Jewish oral traditions that are known as the Oral Torah.
[130] for dogmatic reasons (e.g., 2 Maccabees 12:46 raises the subject of sacrifice offered for the dead).
[131] The Leipzig Debate took place in June and July 1519 at Pleissenburg Castle in Leipzig, Germany. Its purpose was to discuss Martin Luther's teachings and was initiated and conducted in the presence of George, Duke of Saxony, an opponent of Luther. The Leipzig debate became a critical moment in the history of Christendom by which the Protestant and Catholic churches eventually went their separate ways. The public contest led to the division of the western Catholic church.
[132] i.e., excluded from the subsequent short canon.
[133] is a cache of roughly 400,000 pages of manuscript (and some printed) material that accumulated in the worn text repository (Hebrew: geniza) of the Ben Ezra Synagogue in Cairo between the eleventh century and the late nineteenth.
[134] on the eastern edge of the Judean desert in Israel

why, for instance, the Book of Jonah is to be considered part of the Bible, whereas the Shepherd of Hermas is not.

4. The Church is universal, i.e., catholic

The epithet "catholic" is by no means a subsequent attribute of one denomination so that it may be distinguished from the others. Even Saint Ignatius of Antioch (ca. AD 110-117) called the Church "catholic," which was still the only Christian church at that time.

The true Church was founded by Jesus Himself—not by humans. She, the Church, has existed for two thousand years, essentially unaltered. Orthodox churches, and Protestant churches, which have split into tens of thousands of Protestant denominations and continue to divide, evolved as a consequence of the schisms within the Church in the course of history.

The Catholic Church was, indeed, founded by Christ. Ever since then, She has been thriving and growing under the guidance of the Holy Spirit. She is like a giant tree with splendid boughs and leaves. It is well beyond the scope of the human mind to comprehend the immense richness bequeathed to us by Jesus and fostered by the Holy Spirit for two thousand years. Congregations separated from the Catholic Church detract from the original, natural richness of Christianity.

Once a French atheist chanced to enter a church packed with people. Mass was in progress. The voice of the old priest was barely audible, and whatever could be made out from what he was saying came through as mostly nonsensical and uncongenial. This acute-minded unbeliever stood there in shock, saying to himself, "This huge crowd of people cannot be here only because of the priest. There must be something else going on here!"

IX. Sources of Grace

Many find it unacceptable that the Church transmits the power and grace of God through certain practices (Baptism, Confession). But is it possible, after all, that God's power is communicated via human acts?

1. Christ has stayed with us

In giving Himself to the world in Jesus, God did not approach humankind to make a brief presence in our history. He incarnated into history with the intention of making His divine presence accessible to every human being of every age. The Resurrected Christ is alive and acts through those belonging to Him, even today, for He promised: "I will not leave you orphans; I will come to you. In a little while the world will no longer see me, but you will see me, because I live and you will live... you are in me and I in you." (John 14:18-20) "...stay in the city until you are clothed with power from on high" (Luke 24:49). The first Christians lived with the conviction that, among them and in them, the Spirit of the living God was alive and active. Therefore, they called the Church the body of Christ because they believed that His Spirit was in them (1 Corinthians 12:12-13). As for the important decisions made by the Church, Christians were convinced that these were guided by the Holy Spirit. The first Apostolic Council dispatched a letter beginning with the following words to Antioch: "It is the decision of the Holy Spirit and of us..." (Acts 15:28)

2. Christ, the Church, and the sacraments

During the first few centuries of Christianity, one of the most common terms to describe the sacraments was the word *symbolon*. The original meaning of the word was "composite." This was the term applied to denote contracts, for instance, written on a bone fragment, wooden board, or clay tablet, and subsequently broken into two so that each party could receive their piece. When it came to payment (as with a loan), the two pieces were joined together. A snug fit proved that the contract was authentic.

Later, the Greeks would use the expression *symbolon* with reference to symbols or representations, since they were also seen as composite entities, containing something visible (sign) and something invisible (signified). Thus, for example, the visible flag may be an indication of someone's invisible patriotism.

Christians spoke of the sacraments as *symbolon*s (or *symbola* in the plural), because they were also interpreted as a composite: visible signs or gestures communicating invisible divine grace and power.

In some sense, even Christ Himself may be described as a *symbolon* or sacrament, for in Him—a visible and real human being— the invisible and eternal God appeared and acted. Secondly, the Church could also be called a *symbolon* because, in a visible community, the unseen Holy Spirit is present and active. The Church is the body of Christ, as She is defined by the presence of His Spirit. Finally, the Church's basic actions toward individual Christians, i.e., the sacraments, may also be called *symbola*. In them, through a visible act, the Christian believer encounters the living, resurrected Christ Himself. Thus, when somebody is baptized, not only do they join a human community, but they are truly grafted onto the body of the living Christ and share in His redemptive grace, as well.

3. The sacraments are present in the Bible

Though the Church did play an active role in the establishment of the forms of the seven sacraments (Baptism, Confirmation, Eucharist, Confession, Holy Orders—the ordination of priests, Marriage, and the Anointing of the Sick), far from being later inventions of the Church, the sacraments are there in the Bible.

Baptism is present in Jesus's missionary commandment (Matthew 28:19), as well as later in the life of the early Church (Acts 8:36; 10:48; 16:32; Romans 6:1-23). The Sacrament of Confirmation (i.e., the conferment of the power of the Holy Spirit) is, among other things, represented in the account of the conversion of the Samaritans (Acts 8:15-17; 19:1-7; 1 John 2:27). The Eucharist (Jesus giving His Flesh and Blood as food and drink) appears at the Last Supper (Mark 14:22-24), in Jesus's speech in Capernaum (John 6:51-58), and in the liturgies, ceremonies, and prayer life of the early Church (Acts 2:42; 1 Cor. 11:17-34).

At the Last Supper, Jesus did not say, "This bread is *like* My body." Neither did He say, "This bread *will remind you of* My body." What He said was, "Take it; this is My body" (Mark 14:22). In Capernaum, He said: "Amen, amen, I say to you, unless you eat the flesh of the Son of Man and drink his blood, you do not have life within you. Whoever eats my flesh and drinks my blood has eternal life, and I will raise him on the last day. For my flesh is true food, and my blood is true drink. Whoever eats my flesh and drinks my blood remains in me and I in him. Just as the living Father sent me and I have life because of the Father, so also the one who feeds on me will have life because of me." (John 6:53-57)

The mission of the forgiveness of sins is given by the resurrected Christ to the Apostles (John 20:23), and consequently to priests through the laying on of hands in Holy Orders. The apostles, bishops, and priests have exercised the power of binding and loosing, as with the Sacrament of Confession, also called Reconciliation or Penance, from the beginning (1 Cor. 5:3-5). The transfer of apostolic mission and authority by the laying on of hands, as happens in the Sacrament of Holy Orders, may also be found in the pages of the Bible (1 Tim. 4:14; Acts 14:23). The anointing of the sick with oil emerges in the Gospel (Mark 6:13), as well as in the practices of the early Church (James 5:14). Marriage of a man and a woman in a union for life, indissoluble and joined together by God, is mentioned in Jesus's teaching (Mark 10:1-9) and in the letters of Paul the Apostle (Eph. 5:32). Thus, the sacraments are by no means inventions of later times.

4. Faith in the sacraments pervaded the lives of Christians from the beginning

The Church has, from the beginning, lived, believed in, and taught the reality of the sacramental presence of Christ. Saint Ignatius of Antioch (d. ca. AD 110-117), for example, writes the following on the Eucharist: "The Eucharist is the flesh of our Savior Jesus Christ, who suffered for our sins and who, in his goodness, the Father raised" (The Epistle of Ignatius to the Smyrnaeans 7:1). Around AD 155, Saint Justin wrote as follows: "For not as common bread and common drink do we receive these; but in like manner as Jesus Christ our Savior, having been made flesh by the Word of God, had both flesh and blood for our salvation, so likewise have we been taught that the food which is blessed by the prayer of His word, and from which our blood and flesh by transmutation are nourished, is the flesh and blood of that Jesus who was made flesh." (First Apology, LXVI:5) This mystery is captured by Saint John Chrysostom (AD 347-407): "The creative Spirit of God transforms the bread."

The treatise "Traditio Apostolica," presenting the rules of church life of Roman Christianity around AD 215, records the text of the Eucharist (the Mass).[135] This text is essentially identical to the Second Canon of the Mass, as used in the Catholic Church currently. Someone going to a Eucharistic celebration around AD 200 would have been likely to hear almost literally the same Mass prayers as the ones we say in our churches today!

Concerning the practice of penance, Saint Clement of Rome (Bishop of Rome from AD 92-99) noted, "It is better for man to confess his transgressions..." The act of penance and satisfaction was to be determined by the presbyters (cf. Clement of Rome, First Epistle 51:3; 54:1; 57:1). Saint Irenaeus, Bishop of Lyon (d. AD 202), also discussed the practice of public repentance and absolution at length (Adversus Haereses—"Against Heresies" I. 6:3; 13:5.7; III. 3:4; 4:2). Origen (AD

---

[135] Apostolic Tradition (4), likely written by Hippolytus of Rome, revealing the life of prayer, worship and liturgy of the Roman Church in the late 2nd century.

184/185-253/254) reported that each penitent was commended to a priest, hearing his or her confession and accompanying him or her. Once the penance set by the priest had been performed and the accompaniment process was over, the convert could join the ranks of public penitents (Homilies on Leviticus 2:4).

Regarding the Anointing of the Sick, Pope Innocent I (AD 416) clarified in his letter to the Bishop of Gubbio that the anointing of the sick was a sacrament (Enchiridion, p. 216).[136] Saint John Chrysostom (AD 347–407) also remarked that priests anointed the sick for the forgiveness of their sins (De Sacerdotio —"About Priesthood," 3,6).

The manner of ordaining bishops, priests, and deacons is documented even in the Didache (ca. AD 90), as well as, subsequently, in the treatise "Traditio apostolica" (AD 215) (Didache 15,1[137]; Apostolic Tradition 2-3; 7-8).

Christian marriage was described by Tertullian (ca. AD 155–240) in the following way: "...that marriage which the Church cements, and

---

[136] Denzinger, Henry, Hundermann, Peter, *Enchiridion Symbolorum: A Compendium of Creeds, Definitions and Declarations of the Catholic Church* (Ignatius Press: 2012), p. 216.

[137] Didache—"Teaching," also known as The Lord's Teaching through the Twelve Apostles to the Nations, is a brief anonymous early Christian treatise written in Koine Greek, dated by most modern scholars during the first century.

the oblation confirms, and the benediction signs and seals; (which) angels carry back the news of (to heaven), (which) the Father holds for ratified" (Ad Uxorem—a letter "to His Wife" II 8:6).

The handful of highlights above are only meant to give a brief foretaste of what anyone who reads the writings of the first Christians can experience for themselves. The essential sameness of the faith of the first Christians and today's Catholic faith is astonishing.

5. Why have certain sacraments been eliminated from the practice of Protestant churches?

The Catholic Church is cognizant of the fact that Protestant Christianity professes and practices extremely valuable evangelical truths, emphasizing the central position of the Bible, enabling celebration of worship services in the vernacular, proclaiming the precedence of grace over good deeds, etc. The Catholic Church also drew the lessons from these and corrected its one-sided practices and approaches accordingly. In addition, our Church is well aware that the Catholic side is also to be blamed for the Church's schism in the 16th century, so both parties bear the burden of responsibility in this regard.

Having said that, we are of the view that the Protestant Reformers limited the scope of Christian teaching. They tended to be biased toward the importance of the Word of God, the reception of God's Word, and Christ's promise, while somewhat forgetting that God gives His grace through means other than His Word, as well. Not only did God intend to speak to us, but He also became flesh and gives His body to us, aiming to nourish and sustain us through this sacramental reality.

In addition, human forces of inertia have also played a role in the disappearance of certain sacraments from Protestant practice. Luther, for example, would go to Confession until his death; he considered it to be a very important source of grace granted by Christ. He did not seek to abolish the Sacrament of Penance.[138] However, as this sacrament is time-consuming and not always easy to administer, it gradually fell out of use, due to inertia. This abandonment was also reinforced by the radicalization of the teaching on Christ as the sole mediator between human beings and God, precluding His action as mediator in different ways.

---

[138] Martin Luther objected to the mandatory nature of Confession and stressed that the main point in Confession was not the imposition and performance of a particular act of penance but absolution instead. In 1529, Luther encouraged the practice of Confession in several of his speeches and remarked with regret that it was neglected by many. Cf. *Luther's Large Catechism: A Contemporary Translation with Study Questions* (ed. Janzow, F. Samuel; St. Louis, 1978), pp. 122-27.

6. The treasures of Protestantism

Churches of the Protestant Reformation profess and live aspects of Christianity that the Catholic Church has been able to learn from and draw upon because, previously, their significance had diminished in the Catholic tradition. A prime example of these would be the emphasis on the pre-eminence of God's freely given love and grace. One of the most pivotal messages of the Bible may be summed up thus: God loves us freely, in spite of our sins. Furthermore, some other major values of the churches of the Reformation include love and knowledge of the Bible, appreciation of the involvement of lay people in the Church, and the reinstatement of the vernacular in the liturgy.[139] They also made Christianity simpler and less clerical.

Protestant Christianity played a prominent part in fighting slavery, proclaiming the Gospel on non-Christian continents, and mitigating the poverty of those living in the colonies. Protestant churches had a crucial role in building the American nation, and their contribution to the culture of the United States has been enormous. The same is also true for other nations.

For all of these reasons, the Catholic Church regards the churches of the Reformation with gratitude, ready to learn from them, and engage in the dialog of love and truth with various Protestant denominations.

Charles de Foucauld (1858-1916) was born into a wealthy, aristocratic family with an ancient pedigree. At the age of six, he lost both of his parents. As a young military officer, he identified himself as an agnostic, squandered large sums of money on gambling, and frequently organized extravagant banquets, occasionally with girls brought from Paris. In the end, his relatives decided to place him under the care of a guardian to prevent him from causing any more loss for the family. When he learned that his military unit was in combat in Algeria, he enlisted in the army again. He fought bravely. At night, he would spend hours with his eyes fixed on the breathtaking view of the starry sky. He also viewed the faith of the Arabs with admiration. Then, accompanied by a Jewish rabbi, he set out on a rather dangerous exploratory journey to Morocco, a country

---

[139] As is widely known, vernacular translations of the Bible existed even before the Reformation. The first complete German translations of the Bible were made in the 14th century. Their texts were utilized by Martin Luther as well. In the English language, Reformation-period Bible translations, such as Tyndale's Bible (1526), Miles Coverdale's Bible (1535), the Geneva Bible (1560), the Bishop's Bible (1568), and the Authorized King James Version (1611), were preceded by Wycliffe's 14th-century Bible. Although no complete translations of the Bible were produced in the Old English period (ca. 500 - ca. 1100), translations of individual books (e.g., the Book of Psalms) or even larger sections of the Bible (e.g., parts of the Old Testament and the Gospels) survive. The earliest extant translation of the four Gospels into Old English is found in the Lindisfarne Gospels in the form of interlinear glosses (i.e., word-for-word translation of the Latin text inserted between the lines) prepared by Aldred, Provost of Chester-le-Street (10th century).

isolated from the rest of the world, at that time. For the travelogue he wrote, he was awarded a gold medal by the Geographical Society. However, he was tormented by a sense of inner emptiness and restlessness. He rented an apartment in Paris, and along the route of his walks, he would enter a couple of churches more and more often. Churches were the only places where he could experience a sense of emotional well-being. One day, he walked into the Church of St. Augustine, the workplace of his much beloved aunt's confessor, Abbé Huvelin. He went up to him, asking him to teach him about the truths of the Christian religion. He said to the abbé, "I have doubts about my faith. Can I ask you a few questions? Please answer me."

The old priest looked at him, intuitively inferring from his face the tumultuous story of the preceding years, and saw an intense desire for God in him. He finally answered, "Please come into the confessional, kneel down, confess your sins, and you will believe."

But Foucauld replied, "I didn't come to confess my sins. Practically, I don't even believe in God. I have questions. Please answer them." However, the father looked into his eyes again and said, "Confess your sins and you will believe!" In the end, Foucauld yielded to this nagging. He knelt down and laid down the sins of a decade and more at the feet of God, without embellishment or self-justification. At that very moment, he felt the powerful stream of grace flow through his whole being. As soon as he stepped out of that confessional, he believed indeed. Some days later, he decided to become a monk. This is how one of the greatest figures of the 20th century, the saint of the desert, embarked on his mission.[140]

---

[140] Six, Jean-Francois (ed.), *The Spiritual Autobiography of Charles de Foucauld* (Word Among Us, Frederick, MD, 2003), pp. 9-24; Puskely, Maria, *Akik hittek a szeretetben* (Budapest, 1979), pp. 385-393.

X. A Morality That Compromises Freedom?

According to Nietzsche, Christianity poisoned love.[141] By this he meant that humans in antiquity, prior to the emergence of Christianity, had been able to live and celebrate bodily love freely, without misgivings

---

[141] Nietzsche, Frederich, *Jenseits von Gut und Böse* IV, p. 168.

and remorse. Physical beauty was represented in art without any sense of shame. Aphrodite or Venus was positively seen as a deity. Christianity, Nietzsche argued, deprived human beings of this genuine sense of joy. It littered the simplest road to happiness with "do nots," turning it into a guilt trip. Medieval sculptures and paintings show fully buttoned up figures. Christianity vitiated love and would not let people be happy.[142]

Jean-Paul Sartre wrote that, when he was a child, the image of the all-seeing eye of God was instilled in him. Once, he was playing with matches and he dropped a lit match on a nice tablecloth, and it burned a hole in it. Sartre was scared, but when he realized no one had seen the incident, he cheered up. He hastily crumpled up the tablecloth and slid it behind a cupboard. All of a sudden, he was reminded of what had been taught to him about God seeing everything, including his mischief. He thought God had recorded it in His book, and on the day of reckoning, He would bring him to account for his action. As an adult, Sartre noted that he deeply resented this as a small child, which made him question: Who is this God, constantly following close on my heels like a policeman, not leaving me alone in peace, not letting me be free to live on my own, who will one day make me answer for all of my deeds? He resolved to be liberated and not to live with such horrible burdens of conscience. He decided that he would become an atheist.[143]

As a relatively recent proverb has it, anything in life that is any fun is either illegal, immoral, or fattening. In a similar vein, many people believe that Christian morality encroaches on an individual's freedom and makes them unhappy, not letting them live their lives freely. As Nietzsche put it in a rather radical way, it is as if God needed to be killed so that man might be a complete human being.

1. Ten Words of God

What is morality essentially about? Christians firmly believe that morality is not some arbitrary, subjective, cultural product. Morality is essentially about recognizing the orderliness and amazing harmony inherently present in the world and encoded in our cells and souls. People decipher this orderliness from the blueprint of nature and try to live accordingly.

According to an ancient rabbinic teaching, God created the world with ten Words (as in the first Genesis narrative where the phrase "and God said" occurs ten times).[144] Therefore, as the rabbis pointed out, the

---

[142] Cf. Benedict XVI, *Deus caritas est* (2006), pp. 3-4.

[143] Sartre, Jean-Paul, *Les Mots* (Paris, 1964), pp. 78.

[144] *Pirqe Abot*, 5,1. (Pirkei Avot, which translates to *English as Chapters of the Fathers*, is a compilation of the ethical teachings and maxims from Rabbinic Jewish tradition.)

text of the Bible was meant to allude to the Ten Commandments, called "ten Words" or "ten propositions" in Hebrew. What is this rabbinic interpretation intended to emphasize? The fact that God's commandments, the moral commandments, are not some retroactively drafted, arbitrary regulations, but have been imprinted on the universe since the time of creation: on the stars, the instincts of animals, and the human soul. The Ten Commandments, which were recognized and expressed by Moses, are the same as the Ten Commandments by which God created the stars and the cosmos. Morality is but the humble act of inferring from the world which paths, directions, and harmony the Creator has hidden within it so that we may walk on those paths, in those directions, and embrace that harmony in our lives.

2. Do moral laws deprive us of our freedom?

Is morality a straitjacket that limits our freedom of movement and makes us unhappy? Does it deny us the magnificent gifts of individuality and freedom?

What does freedom consist in, after all, and how should it be used? Free decision-making is a capability related to volition, just as judgment formation and proper cognition are abilities of the mind. The mind's ability to think is aimed at truth and reality. Erring makes no one more intelligent. A human being may be described as truly intelligent if he or she never errs, but always uses his or her cognitive abilities to identify whatever is true as true and whatever is real as real. Just as our intelligence is aimed at truth and reality, by the same token, our volitional ability is geared towards what is good and valuable. The more a person wills and chooses what is good, the freer they are. The less an individual's will is fettered by some passion or impulse, the less one is blinded by craving for something bad, the freer one will be. A human being does not become free by choosing what is bad. The more somebody is willing and longing for whatever is good at all times, the more they can soar in faith and love others, the freer they will be.

A soccer player is free, not when he is kicking balls all over the place, but when he can execute a single precise move and shoot the ball to the top right-hand corner of the goal. The more he is able to control his body and focus on right movement, the freer he is.

Freedom is a fragile and narrow path. Moving up on this road means making choices leading to more life. Unfortunately, people today often idolize unchecked experimentation, the chronic avoidance of commitment, and momentarily satisfying options. Thus, all too often, they travel along the highway of death, the rejection of the true and the good, and the degeneration of society.

3. Does an ethical life make one unhappy?

Morality does not compromise human freedom. God's commandments are like road signs; they show the way to life, and to more life. The Evil One is always intent on making us believe that God diminishes our happiness. However, this is not the case. As the Hungarian pastor and psychologist Endre Gyökössy put it, "One woman is more than many women." If somebody finds their significant other and can love and serve that person with all their heart through their whole life, they do not lose, but win happiness.

Saint Irenaeus said, "The glory of God is man fully alive" (Adversus Haereses, 20.7). Rivers praise God by flowing and flowers by blooming. A human being praises God by being alive in the true sense of the word, realizing his or her full potential. God does not begrudge us our happiness but seeks to enable us to be happy and prosper.

Nietzsche's allegation that Christianity poisoned love is a gross misrepresentation of reality. The sexuality cult of antiquity was by no means about the exaltation of true love. Celebrations in that age tended to serve as settings for cultic prostitution and entertainment that devolved into orgies, with paid prostitutes and the pathetic search of intoxicated individuals for pleasure. The Bible and Christianity most categorically condemn these expressions of lust, for far from representing the exaltation of love, they debased and defiled it. Scarcely could today's sexuality cults, pornography, and prostitution be seen as the elevation of love, either.

The Bible and Christianity teach that true love is the way to another human being's personality, to an individual who deserves and demands unconditional and total devotion. True love will very soon give rise to the desire for unconditionality and the complete and irrevocable dedication of one's life to another person in a manner that affects one's full being.

Rather than poisoning love, Christianity positively claims that marriage is a sacrament, a divine reality. Every time that husband and wife in love become one again, in sexual union, it is God Himself, His infinite love, that becomes present in them, and through them, for the world.

The Bible has an entire book that focuses on love: the Song of Songs. Not incidentally, this book also praises bodily love. The Church has canonized a number of married couples, recommending them as exemplary. These couples lived and experienced love at a very high intensity, with utmost generosity and devotion, in truly happy and fulfilling relationships. Some examples are Saint Elizabeth of Hungary (1207-1231), Princess of the Kingdom of Hungary; Landgravine of Thuringia, who loved her husband passionately, as did St. Gianna

Beretta Molla,[145] and the recently beatified Quattrocchi couple, Luigi and Maria Beltrame.

4. Appropriate and inappropriate sense of guilt

Jean-Paul Sartre, whose childhood experience of accidentally burning a tablecloth was mentioned earlier, described guilt as all-consuming, embittering, and stifling. Some forms of guilt are indeed debilitating.

Guilt is appropriate, as long as it serves as an indication of the right path to take, and as long as the pain of remorse spurs one to do what is good.

However, as soon as guilt grows into an enormous, crushing burden, it can no longer be described as Christian or conducive to progress. The biblical name of the Evil One is "Satan," which means "The Accuser" (cf. Zechariah 3:1-5); it is no surprise, then, that accusation is one of his chief tactics. He keeps telling people, "You will never be worthy of a good and joyful life, so you had better not even try." He casts people into the mire. The Bible calls the Holy Spirit *Parakletos*, "The Defender." God seeks to defend, raise up, and purify us. His look and His closeness are never humiliating, but cleansing and elevating.

If somebody is oppressed by inappropriate and all-consuming guilt, they can tell Satan, in their hearts without fear, "I am God's beloved child. He lifts me up and cleanses me of my sins. As for you, be gone!"

Pope Pius XII said that the gravest sin of the contemporary man is that he has lost his sense of guilt.[146] Nowadays, many maintain that there is no such thing as sin, that it is merely the invention of priests. Every effort is made to explain everything with reference to psychological urges and childhood traumas. Interestingly enough, this world, which rejects the notion of sin and denies the existence of the bad, has rather rapidly lost its sense of good, as well: a point of reference for determining what is bad. The possibility of catharsis—in the sense of suddenly releasing the heavy burden of sin—is waning, and the passage from bad to good is also disappearing. As Pope John Paul II wrote, one of the main reasons for the sense of resignation prevalent across Europe these days is the inability to admit sin and ask for forgiveness.[147]

If someone knows that there is such a thing as sin, but also knows there is forgiveness from God with His merciful Heart, then that

---

[145] Molla, Gianna Beretta, Love *Letters to My Husband*, Pauline Books & Media (April, 2002).
[146] Radio message broadcast on October 26, 1946; *Discorsi e Radiomessaggi di Sua Santità Pio XII*, VIII. Ottavo anno di Pontificato, 2° marzo 1946 - 1° marzo 1947, pp. 285-289.
[147] John Paul II, *Ecclesia in Europa* (2003), p. 76.

person will not be afraid to call his or her sins by name, aware of the fact there is a way out of them and reconciliation.

5. Does brute force in evolution correspond to free competition in humanity?

Not infrequently do we hear that the engine of the development of the living world is brute force: the stronger animal eats the weaker one. This is said to have ensured the selection of increasingly more viable genes. Many suggest that the life of humankind ought to be based on this fundamental law: the stronger ones devour the weaker ones! The economy will only be vigorous if free competition is enabled—so the argument goes.

Those thinking in this way seem to be oblivious of the fact that it was not plain brute force that propelled evolution within the animal world. The most aggressive animal species became extinct because they had eaten up their food chain or had killed the other members of their species. It was not the most aggressive, but the most adaptable species, that survived.

A limit to violence appears to emerge even in the animal world. For instance, Arctic wolves often fight for the leading role. When a male loses the combat, he holds out his neck to the winner. However, the victor will not bite through the neck of the vanquished wolf. Thus, there are restrictions on brute force, even in the animal world.

If a human society is predicated upon the law of free competition, that community will soon be full of many unhappy people. In free competition, the weak, the poor, the old, and the infirm, are inevitably left behind. Free competition is the world of the strong, the successful, and the uninhibited, of the kind that would gladly walk over another person's dead body in pursuit of their own happiness. Another reason a society based on free competition generates masses of despondent individuals is because humans were not born to live like this. We were not born to gather and fight for ourselves. Human beings were born to love and give, create and build.[148]

The biblical analogy of society is the human body, not a pyramid with everyone scrambling to reach the peak. We are all one body, brothers and sisters of one another. If one member rejoices, all the members will rejoice with it. If one member suffers, all the members will suffer with it (1 Cor. 12.26). This is God's dream of human coexistence.

---

[148] Pope Francis discusses the subject in a shockingly powerful tone. Cf. Pope Francis, *Evangelii gaudium*, pp. 53-54; Tornielli, Andrea; Galleazi, Giacomo., *This Economy Kills* (Liturgical Press, Collegeville, MN, 2015), pp. 20-21.

6. Some frequently criticized principles of Christian morality

A. Speech

Some people believe that a few obscene expressions or swearwords do no one any harm. They see them as ways to let off steam. However, this is not entirely true. According to an old Latin proverb, speech is the mirror of the soul.[149] Our words come from inside of us, from our mind and heart. Foul language issuing from somebody is a negative signal. It is an indication of something deteriorating within that person, causing them to come across as rude and vulgar. Sometimes words may inflict greater pain than a slap on the face. The Bible aptly puts it like this: "A blow from a whip raises a welt, but a blow from the tongue will break bones" (Sirach 28:17). The lash of a whip hurts only on the outside and leaves a wound on the skin, but words uttered with contempt and hatred penetrate into the inner world of another, possibly crushing them within.

If speech is indeed the mirror of the soul, our western societies show rather impoverished images of themselves.

B. The mystery of romance

Many people consider Christian convictions about marriage and romantic love to be particularly difficult to accept. At the same time, these teachings are highly esteemed by others. For example, in Japan, many non-Christians volunteer to attend pre-Cana marriage preparation courses and request a church wedding.

The Bible unequivocally teaches, and Christianity firmly believes, that marriage is the complete dedication of a man and a woman's life to each other and the full union of two people, with the infinite love of God the Creator, Himself, present and active in it (cf. Genesis 2:23-24; Ephesians 5:32). Bodily union is the most profound way for a married couple to experience their love and unity. This act is true and proper, if it is not only two bodies, but also two human beings that enter into union, celebrating and sealing the harmony of their lives, sharing their pains and joys, their past and future. Otherwise, both parties would feel that they did something that was not fully true. They pretended to be one, but that was not necessarily the case.

Marriage, just as with any other valuable and lofty endeavor in life (e.g., sporting accomplishments, scientific achievements, artistic creations, etc.) is not sustained easily, in a completely effortless way. A good marriage is like a beautiful symphony with two strains. Instead of clashingly interfering with each other's melody, they must work

---

[149] Imago animi sermo est.

very hard for this symphony to sound neat and pleasing to the ear. A good marriage is two human beings' collective masterpiece of almost superhuman proportions.

It is incredibly labor-intensive. At the beginning of a romantic relationship, blissful unity is presented to the couple virtually automatically. Walls separating the two of them come crumbling down. They may step out of the prison of their solitude and enter the marvelous world of the other. They are enabled by each other to receive many things that would have been completely absent from the individual life of each. Precious little needs to be done to secure this mutually enriching unity. Later on, however, two people cannot stay together without effort. Events that take place may be experienced in different ways by the two. Mistakes of varying severity are bound to be made, and even the walls that were previously removed will inevitably have to be rebuilt. Only a marriage in which two people can destroy these re-emerging walls and find each other's hand, time after time, recreating the miracle of unity, will remain fulfilling. All this requires a high degree of sensitivity, good intentions, willingness to start again, forgiveness, humor and inventiveness, combined with quality time and periodic honeymoons.

As Erich Fromm put it: Love is not comparable to possession or indulgence. Love is art. It is an amazing ability to bring forth treasures from myself and my partner, recreating the marvel of unity.[150]

C. Homosexuality

In line with the teaching of the Bible and of Christianity, according to the Creator's design, sexuality is naturally meant to enable a man and woman to experience their love and union and to promote reproduction. Thus, sexual relationships involving same-sex individuals do not agree with the blueprint and purpose of human sexuality given by God at our creation of male and female (Genesis 19:5; Romans 1:26-27).

Therefore, the Church does not deem it appropriate to label the cohabitation of same-sex individuals "marriage," and does not approve of allowing same-sex couples to adopt children.

In doing so, Christianity does not intend to, nor does it condemn people of a homosexual orientation. It does not even regard the orientation itself as a sin, only homosexual acts. Christianity does not seek to stigmatize or discriminate against persons with a homosexual orientation and repudiates the social exclusion or stigmatization of such individuals.

Homosexuality is not an innate, predetermined orientation. This is corroborated by the stories of many pairs of identical twins with

---

[150] From, Erich, *The Art of Loving* (Harper & Brothers, New York, 1956), pp. 9-15. 103-129.

different sexual orientations. Notably, a large number of psychiatrists and physicians are of the opinion that the majority of individuals with a homosexual orientation are not 100% homosexual. Their personalities have a healthy, heterosexual part, and they could choose to give priority to this component of themselves. Once such a decision is made, even despite the difficulties, the individual may experience a true sense of fulfillment in man-and-woman relationships and in marriage.[151]

In 2005, the Parliament of Spain passed legislation recognizing the right of same-sex couples to marriage, including child adoption. When the voting was over, the members of parliament stood up and applauded for several minutes. The scene gave the impression that they had enabled an outstanding accomplishment of civilization. All this suggests that it is no longer necessarily clear for humans living in this age that a man and a woman making love to each other is natural and conducive to life. When same-sex individuals try to do the same, life will fail to result, as something has been broken. It appears as if we do not see even the most objective facts distinctly. Little time passed before Rocco Buttiglione, a man who had graciously, perspicaciously, and firmly criticized the law passed in Spain, was nominated to the position of Commissioner of Home Affairs and Justice of the European Union by the Italian government. The Human Rights Commission of the European Parliament rejected his nomination. Buttiglione became *persona non grata* in the EU—a manifestation of a current tyranny of tolerance. Today, tolerance appears to include intolerance of the worldwide standard institution of marriage between a man and a woman, which goes back thousands of years in human history. Tolerance even includes intolerance of the case that human beings are created male and female.

D. Abortion

The Bible and Christianity are unequivocal that human life begins with conception, a position that happens to be shared by medical science (cf. Exodus 1:17; 21:22; Jeremiah 1:5; Didache 2:2; Epistle to Diognetus 5:6). Whether that life is cut down in the second or sixth month, or disposed of in a trash can after birth, represent only differences in degree. The same human life is destroyed.

Perhaps, one of the reasons why we humans can commit this inhumane atrocity so lightly is that we do not ever see these babies. It is as if our eyes were blindfolded. Were we told to be part of these actions with open eyes and watch the dismembering of the bodies of these children to cause their death on an operating table, most of us would probably never be able to go through with it.

---

[151] Nicolosi, Joseph, *Healing of Homosexuality. Case Stories of Reparative Therapy* (New Jersey, 1997).

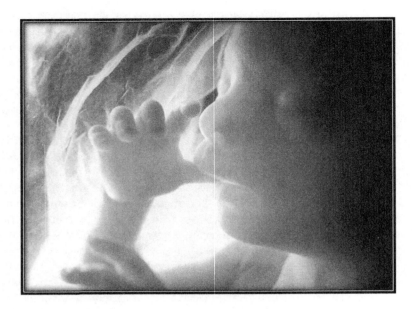

Systematic attempts to remake human language and concepts have in the meantime been made by those who dictate opinion. To further depersonalize the child and the protective role of the parent, they delete the words "father" and "mother" (along with dozens of other names) in "politically correct" language. They talk of "unintended pregnancies," suggesting that it should be the norm that a child's birth is subject to parental approval, and in its absence, the child can be put to death. They use the misnomer "safe abortion" and "reproductive health," both being utterly nauseating terms.[152] After all, what kind of safety or health could abortion offer the child?

In fighting abortion, the Church acts not only in the interest of the child but in the interest of the mother and father. Abortion is an immense wound to the soul of the mother, father, and those involved.[153]

E. Euthanasia

The Bible and Christianity teach that the earthly life of a human being should end with natural death (cf. Deuteronomy 32:39; Job 2:9-10; Book of Wisdom 16:13; Romans 14:7; Saint Augustine, *De civitate Dei* 1:17). Even in the midst of a multitude of afflictions, one human life is of infinite value.

Once, a man in a hospital approached the doctor with the request

---

[152] Peeters, Marguerite A., *The New Global Ethic: Challenges for the Church* (Ominis Terra, 377, 2007), pp. 218, 222.
[153] For a healing retreat for women and men who have experienced abortion, see www.rachelsvineyard.org.

that he facilitate the dying process of his long-suffering mother. The doctor nodded and filled a syringe with a large amount of morphine. The two of them approached the woman's bedside, and the doctor stuck the needle into her skin, but he did not inject the morphine into her body. Instead, he said to the man, "You should inject it."

The man was taken aback: "Should I kill my mother?"

"Why not?" asked the doctor. "Would you have been more comfortable watching *me* killing her?"

A human being is not an animal to be put to sleep so that it will not suffer. At the same time, the Church also teaches that a human being has the right to die with dignity. Medical science ought to avoid overtreating patients. A patient cannot be forced to have his or her life extended as long as possible by means of artificial and extraordinary instruments. The individual has the right not to consent to certain extraordinary treatments, thereby opting for a natural death.

F. The tortures of clerical celibacy

The Catholic Church does not coerce anybody into celibacy. This form of life is freely chosen and accepted by those individuals concerned. This radical form of dedication to God is present not only in the Catholic Church. Buddhist monks, for example, live the same experience. Curiously, they are not attacked or pestered routinely on these grounds.

Celibacy is not torturous. This was the form of life in which Christ, Himself, the most loving and loveable person ever on this Earth, also lived. The Prophet Jeremiah (Jeremiah 16:2), Jesus's mother, Mary (Luke 1:34; Mark 6:3), Paul the Apostle (1 Corinthians 7:7; 9:5), Luke and John also lived in celibacy, along with countless other Christians from the first centuries to the present. Before any ordinance on celibacy was issued, prior to the evolution of the first monastic communities, both men and women in large numbers had chosen a celibate life. Christianity produced a book in praise of virginity and chastity earlier than on marriage.[154] Jesus lit a fire on Earth, and its flames flared up very quickly.

I would rather not embark on theoretical explanations as to why the Catholic Church looks upon celibacy as a valuable asset and as fit for the priesthood. Indeed, why someone surrenders his most intimate privacy and his whole being cannot be explained in purely rational terms. Neither can romantic love be justified through logical reasoning. A person with a divine calling feels that he cannot offer God, Who gave His very Self fully to mankind, anything less than himself, either. He responds to the folly of the Cross with the folly of celibacy.

Celibacy is a sign. It proclaims that God is real; He can fill the entire life and heart of a real flesh-and-blood human being with Himself. It

---

[154] Methodus of Olympus, *Symposium*. This work was written in the late 3rd century.

is no coincidence, therefore, that the Evil One fiercely opposes this sign from within, through the priest's or the religious person's own weaknesses, as well as from without, through attacks from the world and the denigration of this noble calling.

Celibacy also liberates a person for the service of others. Throughout history, such dedicated lives have yielded love, service, and fruit beyond measure. Among these, we find Saint Mother Teresa of Calcutta, Saint Damien De Veuster of Moloka'i, the apostle of lepers, and Saint Maximilan Kolbe, who sacrificed his life for a fellow prisoner in Auschwitz—to mention only three out of the many.

7. The social teaching of Christianity

The Bible and Christianity unequivocally teach that humans are essentially social beings, naturally organizing themselves into societies and states (cf. Deuteronomy 17:14-20; Romans 13:1-7). There are values that human beings can only realize jointly, through social cooperation. Rather than maintaining the power of the ruling classes, the state is supposed to serve the common good. The common good denotes the physical, mental, and spiritual conditions conducive to the development of the individual's human potential (e.g., road networks, public safety, education, health care, culture, etc.).

Christianity also firmly believes that the economy is not to be governed only by free competition. According to the logic of free competition, the strong and the rich are in a position to use their economic superiority against the weak and the poor. The job of the state is to regulate the economy in line with the fundamental principles of justice.

Christianity supports the idea of private property, as it guarantees the freedom of the individual. If a person has a private sphere where they can act as they deem best and over which they may exercise full control, that ensures freedom for the individual (as well as for the community). Therefore, the Catholic Church rejects the ideology of communism.

At the same time, Christianity teaches that the right to private property is not without limitations. For instance, an economic system with land ownership concentrated in the hands of very few in a country that primarily lives off agriculture is obviously not appropriate. The world's resources are the works of the Creator and designed to enable everyone on Earth, including future generations, to thrive.[155] Currently, perhaps the most serious problem of the world economy is that the distribution of wealth has reached a hitherto unprecedented level of concentration.[156] The profit of the world economy is concentrated in the hands of just a few, while the majority of humankind and most states struggle to survive. This situation is at the root of a series of crises of various magnitudes. At the moment, one of the weightiest tasks ahead of humanity is to establish, and subsequently enforce, the limits of the right to property.

8. A humanity without morality?

Morality is the fascinating divine orderliness and harmony encoded into the world. It is about experiencing and perceiving the Good in the depths of one's heart. It is an upward lifting gravitational force, the force of the Creator.

---

[155] This is called the principle of the universal destination of goods. Cf. *Compendium of the Social Doctrine of the Church* (Dublin, 2005), Point 177; John Paul II, *Laborem Exercens* 14; Second Vatican Council, *Gaudium et Spes* 69.

[156] Fridrich, Róbert, *Globalizáció és környezet* (Budapest, 2002), p. 4: "As reported by Forbes, the wealth of the 200 richest is in excess of the annual income of 41% of the world's population (2.4 billion people)" (translated from the Hungarian original). A research project conducted at the University of Zurich, Switzerland, has found that a dominant portion of the world economy is managed by approximately 147 companies, Cf. Waugh, Rob; "Does one super-corporation run the global economy?" *Daily Mail*, October 20, 2011.

It is this Force that enables *humans* to rise above their selfishness and limitations and to be generous and magnanimous. Without it, they would collapse, sink into the mire, and live without ideals and conscience.

It is this Force that enables married couples to overcome their finiteness, grievances, and limitations. As long as two people attempt to create a sense of harmony through sheer human effort on a human level only, they will inevitably run into their limitations: the barriers of their comprehension, adaptability, and affection. Only if that mysterious Third One, the tip of the triangle, is present in their marriage, raising both of them above their limitations and grievances, will they be able to discover and rediscover harmony at this higher level.

A society is viable if its members observe certain norms of living together, not only because these are determined by the majority, representing a momentary balance of power, but because its people are convinced that this is, indeed, the right way to live. If a legal system is not fortified with the power of morality, it will need to be buttressed by a succession of statues; left to its own devices, that legal system is bound to collapse. In the end, it will inescapably implode. A police officer cannot be assigned to each and every person to watch over them. A society will thrive if its members believe that its norms of living together are valid and just, providing them with a reason to adhere to them. A genuine legal system laying any claim to this call must be a humble, earthly projection of the objective divine order that the Creator programmed into the world and the human soul.

The following story happened in Germany at the end of World War II. A young man by the name of Karl Fischer was put on a train along with hundreds of other men, bound for Siberia. On a slip of paper, the young man was able to write where he was being taken and that he loved his wife. He addressed the small letter to his wife in Berlin, placed it in a matchbox, and threw it out of the train. Around a week later, when their train had been delayed at a faraway railroad station for days, he became aware of an odd sound. Somebody was walking around the cars, knocking on the wheels outside and then asking quietly, "Is Karl Fischer here?" Karl felt as if he had been hit by a thunderbolt. His comrades lifted him onto their shoulders so that he could look out of the tiny window opening at the top of the boxcar. He saw his wife standing by the railroad car, dressed in railroad uniform. She said to him, "Karl, cheer up! I'll wait for you!" Then the woman started to back off for fear their conversation might be registered by someone. The man watched his wife mesmerized. When his fellow deportees set him down from the roof opening, he was unspeakably happy and could hardly say a word. Later, he would tell the story of his wife countless times, describing what she was like, guessing how she could have received the letter, how she might have been walking over 60 miles, exposing herself to no small danger, to the station from where the trains bound for Siberia were rounded up and where she would eventually find her husband. His comrades literally relished listening to the account. They envied him having such a wife. When, subsequently in Siberia, brought down by disease, he was on the point of giving up his fight for survival, the men would always remind him, "You have to live. You must go home to a woman like that!" During four years of captivity, that woman was an angel of hope for all of them.[157]

---

[157] Hoffsümmer, Willi, *Kurzgeschichten* 7 (Mainz, 2003), pp. 33-35.

Dear Reader,

Is it possible that you also wish for such a spouse? Could Christian morality prove to be not so foolish after all?

XI. Crusades, the Inquisition, and the Rest...

1. "It would be better for him if a great millstone were put around the neck and he were thrown into the sea."

In speaking of the weaknesses, errors, and sins of Christianity and of the Church, first and foremost, it is important to see clearly that these are, in fact, nothing short of scandal, self-contradiction, and pain. Jesus said, "Whoever causes one of these little ones who believe [in me] to sin, it would be better for him if a great millstone were put around his neck and he were thrown into the sea" (Mark 9:42). If a person who believes in God claims that he or she reveres the God of love while performing inhumane deeds, that is scandalous, extremely painful, and outrageous.

Thus, it is not uncommon to find criticism of false religiosity in the Bible. The prophets continually excoriated that kind of religiosity that was compatible with the oppression of the poor and immorality (cf. Isaiah 58:1-12; Amos 5:21-27). On many occasions, Jesus would challenge the false religiosity of the Pharisees, who disdained others and consumed the possessions of widows, while pretending to go out of their way to say their prayers (Matthew 23:1-36).

The sins committed by Christians and by priests, in particular, represent one of the gravest afflictions and wounds of the Church. Our first reaction to these is the act of asking God and people for their forgiveness, as Pope Saint John Paul II did in the 2000 Jubilee year.

2. Black Legend

When, in the 16th century, England and Spain fought for power over the seas and the New World, the English came to adopt defamatory propaganda as one of their chief instruments of warfare. They depicted Spaniards as bloodthirsty and greedy oppressors and disseminated false rumors about them, thereby legitimizing British pirate attacks and raids. In Spain, this anti-Spanish propaganda acquired a name of its own before long: *leyenda negra* (black legend).

This smear campaign continues to have an impact in the present time, as well. The image of the ruthless Spanish conquistador exterminating Native Americans is still fresh in most people's minds. Indeed, some of the Spanish conquerors were cruel. It is notable, however, that in the areas conquered by the Spanish, Native American populations numbering millions have survived and retained their languages to the present day (e.g., Quechua, Aymara and Guarani). On the other hand, in regions where the English appeared on the scene as conquerors, nearly all Native American peoples became extinct and vanished from the stage of history.

In the United States, with its history of British colonialism, the Native American populations have largely lost their indigenous languages. For instance, the largest community of Native American-language speakers in the United States (with a population of only 200,000) is the Navajos. For comparison, the total Native American population in the U.S. currently stands at approximately 2.4 million. By contrast, in Central and South America, a vast number of indigenous peoples and languages have survived. The number of speakers of the Quechua language alone, for example, is approximately 8-10 million.[158] History books, however, continue to focus exclusively on the cruelties of the Spanish (Catholic) conquerors.

These days, one of the main targets of historical revisionism is the Catholic Church. There are many who even deploy enormous financial resources in their effort to undermine the foundations of the Christian faith and weaken the moral authority of the Church through movies and by other means.[159]

Thus, in the following section, as would seem appropriate, the most common accusations against the Church are presented within realistic historical perspectives and explained with relevant historical facts.

3. The most common charges

A. The Crusades

With Mohamed's appearance on the stage of world history (AD 622), the Arabs became a powerful nation of global conquerors. Within a few decades, they subjugated large swathes of the Middle East (AD 638), North Africa, and Hispania (AD 711). This was followed by a comparatively peaceful period of Christian and Muslim coexistence.

About 350 years later, in addition to the devastation of thousands of Christian churches, the Caliph Al-Hakim[160] (AD 996-1021) ordered the tomb of Jesus, the Holy Sepulcher of Jerusalem, to be destroyed; he also made it extremely difficult for Christians to go on pilgrimages to the Holy Land. Meanwhile, the Seljuk Turks made significant advances in Asia Minor and set the capture of Constantinople as their goal. At that time, Byzantine Emperor Alexios I Komnenos sent a delegation to Pope Urban II to request the help of the Western world (AD 1095).

---

[158] Cf. Bartusz-Dobosi, László, *Jezsuiták és conquistadorok harca az indiánokért a XVII-XVIII. Században* (Budapest, n.d.).

[159] To mention only the most well-known of these: Brown, Dan, *The Da Vinci Code* (New York City, 2003); the play, "The Deputy" by Hochhuth, Rolf (1963); Obed Golan's archeological forgeries, etc. Cf. Hesemann, Michael, *Die Dunkelmänner* (St. Ulrich, Augsburg, 2007), pp. 22-23.

[160] In Arabic, his name means "Ruler by God's Command." Caliph Al-Hakim was the sixth ruler of the Egyptian Shiʿi Fatimid dynasty, noted for his eccentricities and cruelty.

It was in response to this appeal that Western Christianity decided to launch military campaigns to liberate the sacred places. During the Crusades, crusaders committed many atrocities, as well. When they occupied Jerusalem (AD 1099), they murdered a large proportion of its inhabitants.[161] In 1187, following the Battle of Hattin, Saladin, the Muslim sultan of Egypt and Syria, exterminated the inhabitants of Mount Tabor and Nazareth in a similar manner. In 1096, in the region of the Rhine, a crusading army massacred Jewish communities in many places, attempting to extort money. Meanwhile, the bishops of

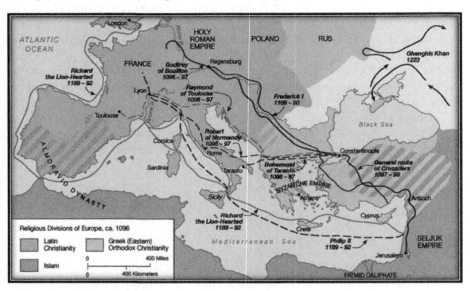

Speyer, Worms, Mainz, Trier, and Cologne, were trying to protect Jewish communities from the mass frenzy of a fanaticized army, but to no avail.

In return for transporting the army, the Venetians demanded from the crusaders the occupation of the Adriatic city of Zara (today's Zadar, Croatia), and subsequently that of Constantinople (AD 1204). In Constantinople, the crusaders killed many and ransacked and desecrated churches.

The Crusades were inspired by Western Christians' religious zeal and their intentions to protect sacred sites and Eastern Christians. Had there not been these campaigns, Eastern Europe would probably have been exposed to Islamic occupation approximately 400 years earlier, which likely would have wiped out European Christianity.[162]

---

[161] The population of Jerusalem, at the time, was approximately 10,000. Prior to the siege, the crusaders granted safe conduct to the residents of the city.

[162] Flaig, Egon, "Der Islam will die Welteroberung," *Frankfurter Allgemeine Zeitung* (2006), p. 120.

B. The Inquisition

Shortly after the turn of the first millennium, certain false teachings were turning into mass movements. Seeing this, Emperor Frederick Barbarossa asked the Pope to take appropriate countermeasures. Accordingly, Pope Lucius III (AD 1184) ordered the examination of heresies (the word "inquisition" refers to such examination), with local bishops in charge of the process. Later, in AD 1231, this responsibility was assigned to the Dominican Order. For the duration of the proceedings, torture was permitted (AD 1252) on condition that injuries causing bleeding were avoided and no permanent harm was induced. The Church oversaw the proceedings, and the sentence was executed by secular authorities.[163] During the entire operation of the Spanish Inquisition (which lasted until the 17th century), as many as 44,000 heresy proceedings were conducted, with the death sentence pronounced in 3000 cases.[164] This totaled around 7 deaths each year that the Inquisition was in existence. Throughout the operation of the Roman (Papal) Inquisition (approximately 400 years), with its jurisdiction covering the whole of Italy, fewer than 50 death sentences were executed.[165]

While heretics were executed and persecuted by kings and cities, often against the objection of church leaders,[166] the Inquisition was a crime against freedom of conscience, human dignity, and the lives of many. It was one of the major mistakes of the Church, albeit at the insistence of monarchs, to aid and abet proceedings against false teachers.

C. Witch-hunt

The pagan peoples of antiquity and the Middle Ages believed in the existence of witches. Civil Roman law stipulated burning alive as a punishment for witchcraft. Similarly, pagan Germanic tribes also believed in the existence of witches and evil sorcery. In these tribes, a person thought to be a witch would be burned.

---

[163] The name of the character, Bernard Gui, in the novel *The Name of the Rose* by Umberto Eco is associated with 42 death sentences.
[164] Kamen, Henry, *The Spanish Inquisition* (New Haven, 2014), p. 253; Hesemann, Michael, *Die Dunkelmänner* (St. Ulrich, Augsburg, 2007), p. 169.
[165] Hesemann, Michael, *Die Dunkelmänner* (St. Ulrich, Augsburg, 2007), p. 173.
[166] The first such tragic case was the execution of a Christian teacher by the name of Priscillian, charged with heresy, at the order of Maximus, usurper of the imperial, in AD 385. The execution was protested by contemporary church leaders, including the Pope and Saint Martin of Tours. Likewise, against the vehement protest of church.

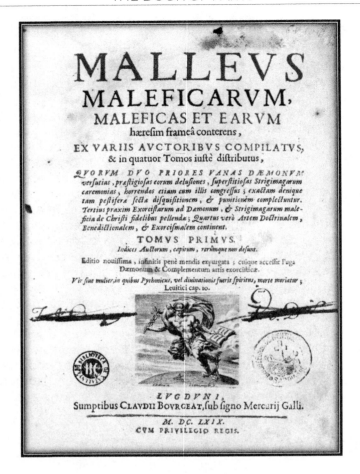

Initially, Christianity condemned belief in the existence of witches and forbade their persecution (Council of Paderborn, AD 785; Pope Gregory VII, AD 1073-1085).

The Church became implicated in witch trials mainly during the activities of the German inquisitor, Heinrich Kramer (AD 1430-1505). His work entitled *Hammer of Witches* (or *Malleus Maleficarum* in Latin) represents a pitiable mixture of insanity and fanaticism. Kramer, alone, was responsible for sentencing 200 women charged with witchcraft to death.

At the same time, it must be noted that belief in the reality of witches infected a large part of contemporary society at the time, especially in the region of the Alps. There were many cases where people reported themselves to the authorities. In a number of instances, the Church intervened in order to save individuals incriminated by secular leaders. For example, in 1654, fifteen children indicted in Lucerne, Switzerland, were successfully transferred to the jurisdiction of the Inquisition of Milan. In Milan, the Church accommodated the children with families, and money was provided for their education. In 1711, the local parish priest in Savognin, Switzerland, attempted to defend four children accused of witchcraft by secular authorities by seeking to pass the case to the jurisdiction of the Inquisitor of Como, Italy. However, due to the unwillingness of the Swiss officials, the two older girls were executed, while their younger peers were poisoned by their own parents. It is also remarkable that individuals charged with witchcraft, on many occasions asked to be tried not by a secular court but by the Church's Inquisition, a considerably more humane and rational ecclesiastical court.

According to estimates, approximately 40,000 people were executed on charges of witchcraft in the whole of Europe. Out of these, there were fewer than one thousand who were sentenced to death by ecclesiastical courts. The rest were convicted by secular courts (those of cities and monarchs). The majority of the executions did not take place in Catholic, but in Protestant areas. Oddly, posterity still blames the Catholic Church for the witch purges.[167]

In an effort to ruin the reputation of the Catholic Church, Hitler ordered a large-scale investigation into the witch purges. Confronted by the aforementioned facts at the end of the inquiries, he decided to relinquish his idea of launching a smear campaign.[168]

It is important to view these events within their own context and milieu. Nonetheless, witch-hunts represent a cause of disgrace in European history, as well as in the history of the Church.

D. The sins of the Catholic Church in the schisms

Schisms are against the will of Christ. His intention was that there would be one flock and one shepherd (John 10:16; John 17:21). However, the Catholic Church also bears the guilt of the schisms.

Prior to the East-West Schism (AD 1054), under imperial pressure, the Pope (AD 1014) included the word *Filioque*, i.e., the doctrine that the Holy Spirit proceeds from the Father and the Son, in the text of the Niceno-Constantinopolitan Creed.[169] Eastern Christians were

---

[167] Cf. Schwerhoff, Gerd., "Vom Alltagsverdacht zur Massenverfolgung. Neuere deutsche Forschungen zum frühneuzeitlichen Hexenwesen," *Geschichte in Wissenschaft und Unterricht* 46 (1955), pp. 359–380; Hesemann, Michael, *Die Dunkelmänner* (St. Ulrich, Augsburg, 2007), pp. 178-194; Cf. Merzbacher, Friedrich, "Hexenprozeß," *Lexikon für Theologie und Kirche* 5 (ed. Höfer, Josef; Rahner, Karl; Freiburg im Bresgau, 1986), pp. 316-319; Mikat, Paul, "Inquisition," *Lexikon für Theologie und Kirche* 5 (ed. Höfer, Josef; Rahner, Karl; Freiburg im Bresgau, 1986), pp. 698-702.
[168] Cf. Hesemann, Michael, *Die Dunkelmänner* (St. Ulrich, Augsburg, 2007), pp. 188-189.
[169] This had been preceded by some related developments. The "Quicumque vult" (ca. AD 500), as well as, subsequently, the Third Local Council of Toledo (AD 589) were the first to incorporate the *Filioque* into the text of the creed. The Council of Friuli acted in like manner (AD 796-797). Cf. Denzinger-Hünermann, *Enchiridion symbolorum definitionum et declarationum*, pp. 75, 617.

justified in their objection to the Pope modifying one of the most significant foundational documents of the Church without convening a council and consulting with them. The barbaric conduct of the crusaders in Constantinople in 1204, followed by the creation of the Latin Empire, made the East-West Schism of 1054 final.

During the events of the Western Schism (AD 1517) of the Protestant Reformation, almost 500 years later, a series of sins and omissions were committed on the Catholic side, as well. Martin Luther did not have a real partner to dialog with. Had the Catholic Church admitted the abuse surrounding the sale of indulgences and paid heed to Luther's justifiable suggestions (e.g., giving the Bible in the vernacular to the faithful or highlighting the precedence of grace over good deeds), in due course, the schism of the Western Church might have been avoided.

E. "Hitler's Pope"

Since the publication of "The Deputy," a play by Rolf Hochhuth, abounding in historical distortions and lies (1963), public opinion has, in part, tended to accuse Pope Pius XII of inaction during World War II by not speaking up to save the Jews.[170] The playwright, Rolf Hochhuth, was a former Hitler Youth member (Hitlerjugend). According to a report by Ian Mihai Pacepa, a former Romanian Secret Service General, Hochhuth was backed by the KGB. The KGB, having collected data on Pius XII between 1960 and 1962, discovered their suitable puppet in Berlin in 1963—Hochhuth, and commissioned him to write a play that would be put on stage in many countries around the world.[171]

In reality, Pope Pius XII made his voice heard in condemnation of Nazism and racism on a number of occasions. In his first encyclical (October 30, 1939), he wrote so firmly about his opposition to Nazism that the Allied Forces would throw down thousands of copies of it from airplanes over Germany. Statements against Hitler would often cost thousands, even tens of thousands of innocent lives. In 1942, as an example, in response to a pamphlet issued by the Archbishop of Utrecht, Holland, condemning Nazism, Hitler ordered the extermination of baptized people of Jewish descent in the Netherlands. Among many others, Edith Stein[172] fell victim to this action.

Pius XII personally sheltered nearly three-thousand Jews in his

---

[170] Blet, Fr. Pierre, *Pius XII and the Second World War: According to the Archives of the Vatican* (Paulist Press, Mahwah, New Jersey, 1999); Wolf, Hubert, *Pope and Devil: The Vatican's Archives and the Third Reich* (Belknap Press, Cambridge, Massachusetts, 2012).

[171] Cf. Hesemann, Michael, *Die Dunkelmänner* (St. Ulrich, Augsburg, 2007), pp. 243-247.

[172] Edith Stein was a German Jewish philosopher who converted to Christianity and became a Discalced Carmelite nun. She was canonized as a martyr and saint of the Catholic Church; she is also one of six patron saints of Europe.

Castel Gandolfo residence. After the World War, the Chief Rabbi of Rome, Israel Zolli, decided to be baptized and adopted the pope's name, Eugenio, as an expression of his gratitude for everything Pope Pius XII did during the World War to save the Jews.[173]

In many places, the Church offered help by issuing forged safe conduct passes and certificates of baptism. Catholics would often risk their own lives by hiding the persecuted in monasteries and private houses. According to estimates by historians, the Catholic Church (nuncios, religious orders, and the Catholic faithful) saved the lives of hundreds of thousands of Jews during World War II.[174]

The Allied Forces were in possession of reliable information about the existence of death camps as of 1943, as well as accurate photographs of the camps from August 1944. Nonetheless, they refused to start bombing railroad lines to Auschwitz.

F. James, son of Joseph and brother of Jesus

Historical Revisionism has not only been guilty of magnifying the sins of Christianity and distorting facts, but has additionally undermined the trustworthiness and historical foundations of the Gospel. The following example could illustrate the point: the sensational news that an ossuary (a chest containing bones) dating from the period of Jesus was found in Jerusalem, went viral in 2002. The inscription on the ossuary read: "James, son of Joseph and brother of Jesus." The inscription suggested that the chest probably contained the bones of James from the Gospels, a relative of Jesus's. As it was argued by many, this text served to prove that Jesus had siblings, and their genetic father was Joseph (contrary to the accounts given in the Gospels).

A couple uncertainties in relation to the find were the location of the discovery, which was obscure, and the fact that it was divulged to the public by an intermediary. The ossuary was later presented at a conference in Canada, where experts were able to view it directly. It was soon ascertained that the second half of the inscription (the words "brother of Jesus") was an ingeniously contrived forgery.[175] The quest to establish the origins of the find was on. It was not long before

---

[173] Cf. Cabaud, Judith, *Eugenio Zolli, Prophète d'un monde nouveau* (Paris, 2002).
[174] Cf. Pollard, John, *The Papacy in the Age of Totalitarianism, 1914-1958* (Oxford, 2014), pp. 341; Lapomarda, V.A., *The Jesuits and the Third Reich* (New York City, 2005), p. 3; Rittner, Carol; Smith, Stephen D.; Steingeldt, Irena, *The Holocaust and the Christian World* (Continuum Intl. Pub. Group, London and New York City, 2000), pp. 234-265. Although the estimate (860 thousand) proposed by Pinchas Lapide, a Jewish diplomat and historian, is considered to be exaggerated by some, it well illustrates the scale of the effort to save human lives. Cf. Siddiqui, H., "Vatican's role in the Holocaust," *Toronto Star*, July 26, 2001; Fischel, Jack R., *Historical Dictionary of the Holocaust* (Lanham-Toronto, 2010), pp. 42-46.
[175] This was subsequently confirmed by the test done by the Israel Antiquities Authority, exposing the unevenness in the shapes of the letters, the artificiality of the patina, as well as other tell-tale features.

investigators found an antiquity manufacturing workshop in Ramat Gan, with a person by the name of Obed Golan, who made "antiquities" (including the similarly infamous Jehoash Inscription). Also found in the workshop were the book and the very pages from which Obed Golan had copied the concluding words and letters of the inscription onto the ossuary—no doubt dating from the time of Christ, but featuring only the initial words of the inscription.[176] The denouncement of the inscription as forgery failed to attract world-wide attention.

G. The sins of priests

One of the gravest pains of the Catholic Church is the sins committed by her priests. A priest who proclaims the Gospel of Christ shoulders greater responsibility. He is supposed to be a messenger of the love of God. It is therefore deeply painful, scandalizing, and saddening if a priest becomes a slave to passions, sins, avarice, sensuality, aggression, or hunger for power.

The sexual abuse of minors perpetrated by a number of priests has been particularly painful over the past decades. Jesus's saying quoted above is especially applicable here: "It would be better for him if a great millstone were put around his neck and he were thrown into the sea" (Mark 9:42). How much harm and suffering such crimes have afflicted on the victims! What damage and ignominy for Christianity!

The revelation of these crimes to the press began in the United States in 2002. It became apparent that many priests had been involved in perpetrating sexual crimes against minors for years on end. The triggering event was the exposure of the story of a priest named John Geoghan, under psychological treatment on multiple occasions, who had committed sexual offenses to approximately 130 boys in 30 years before he was finally sent to prison. In the following months, a long series of similar cases, albeit not claiming so many victims, came to light.[177] Incidents of a comparable nature emerged in other countries, as well (Ireland, Germany, etc.).

The Church is unequivocal in its condemnation of all crimes of this type. In the past, certain senior clergymen in some countries failed to act with due determination in such cases. Currently, church regulations expressly mandate that, should a priest, catechist or other church employee be reasonably suspected of such acts, they must be disqualified from all manner of ecclesiastical service immediately. Subsequently, the individual is to be sanctioned according to the relevant laws of the land.

---

[176] Rahmani, L. Y., *Catalogue of Jewish Ossuaries in the Collection of the State of Israel* (Nos. 396, 570, 573).
[177] Weigel, George, *The Courage to be Catholic: Crisis, Reform, and Future of the Church* (2002, New York City), pp. 9-19.

At the same time, it is also important for us to notice that the ratio of priests and religious among sexual offenders is insignificant, far below their proportion within the entire population. Most cases of sexual assault (approximately 75% of this category of criminality) are perpetrated by family members. In the United States, approximately 15% of students report having been sexually harassed by teachers during their studies. In the United States, 2-3% of Protestant pastors have been accused of sexual misconduct at some point in their lives. A report issued by Christian Ministry Resources (CMR) in 2002 stated that, contrary to popular opinion, there are more allegations of child sexual abuse in Protestant congregations than Catholic ones, and that sexual transgressions are most often committed by volunteers rather than by priests themselves.[178] In Germany, approximately 210,000 sexual offenses against minors were on the radar of the police between 1995 and 2010. Out of these, only 94 involved Catholic Church employees (religious, priests, or laity) as perpetrators. The Catholic Church has around 600,000 employees in Germany (approximately 1.8% of all employees). *All this goes to show that the Church is one of the safest places for children.* According to the calculations of German criminal psychologist H. L. Kröber, non-celibate individuals tend to become perpetrators of sexual offenses by a ratio of 36 to 1, compared to those living in celibacy.[179] Nevertheless, the media focuses on Catholic priests, giving the public the impression that they are the greatest perpetrators, completely contrary to statistics.

4. A sinful and holy Church

The Church is not without its faults. Therefore, every one of us may find their place in it. This is a Church in progress. However, it is not at all one of the most sordid institutions of history. Quite the contrary, humankind owes much to the Church.

Gladiator games in Rome were brought to an end by the Christians.[180] They put a ban on infanticide—so common in antiquity—and helped widows and orphans. The Christian way of thinking contributed to the abolition of slavery.[181] Free schooling and hospitals

---

[178] Clayton, Mark "Sex abuse spans spectrum of churches," *The Christian Science Monitor* (2002). "Perhaps more startling, children at churches are accused of sexual abuse as often as are clergy and staff. In 1999, for example, 42 percent of alleged child abusers were volunteers, about 25 percent were paid staff members (including clergy) and 25 percent were other children."

[179] Kröber, H.L. "Man wird eher vom Küssen schwanger, als vom Zölibat pädophil," *Cicero* (2010).

[180] Telemachus (4th century).

[181] It was repeatedly protested by popes (including Eugene IV, 1435; Paul, 1537). In the territories of the British Empire, it was thanks to the Christianity-inspired abolitionist movement of David Wilberforce that slavery was ended in 1834.

are Christian inventions.[182] Christianity gave rise to the world's first university. The notion of the separation of state and church also originates in the Bible.[183] It was the Christian view of the world that birthed European culture, giving a rocket boost to the development of science.[184] The Christian conviction that every human being is made in God's image enabled the evolution of the modern democratic state structure, legal system, and social network. Had it not been for Christianity, Europe as we know it and western civilization could not have emerged.

Without Christianity, there would have been no Michelangelo, Bach, Mozart, or Thomas Mann. Without Christianity, there would have been no Saint Francis of Assisi, no Saint Mother Teresa of Calcutta, no Dietrich Bonhoeffer, no De Gasperi, no Martin Luther King, no Desmond Tutu, no Pope Saint John Paul II and no Saint Frances Cabrini either. And these names are only the tip of the iceberg. At a grass-root level, acts of love, moving examples of family life, and manifestations of popular piety might not abound if the Gospel did not exist![185]

After all, is this not what really matters when we look at the Church?

The Power and the Glory

The setting of the novel by Graham Greene is Mexico with its volcanoes, bleak villages and towns, vast jungles and uninviting barrenness. Crime is rampant in the tropical heat. Driven by the conviction that the indigenous tribes of the jungles and the poor of the cities would be happier without God and the Church, the ruling regime, called Power, launches a merciless campaign of religious persecution. Persecution inevitably results in martyrdom. Thus, the novel is also a story of martyrdom, but without the devoutness and mysticism of martyrology. The protagonist is a priest: sinful, unclerical, alcoholic, and licentious. Still, he becomes a martyr and gains the grace earned through the afflictions of conscience. He is afraid of

---

[182] *If God Made the Universe, Who Made God?* (Nashville, 2012), p. 28; *Is God Just a Human Invention?* (ed. McDowell, S. - Morrow, J.; Grand Rapids, 2010), pp. 228. The first hospital was established by Bishop Saint Basil the Great in Caesarea in Cappadocia, in 369.

[183] *Is God Just a Human Invention?* (ed. McDowell, S. - Morrow, J.; Grand Rapids, 2010), pp. 224.

[184] The unprecedentedly rapid advances in natural sciences have been largely driven by the emergence of the conviction that the material world is part of Creation. Rather than the dwelling place of the divine, it is a splendid garden that man must work and keep (Gen. 2:15). In other words, humans have a responsibility to explore the material world, subject it to their control by taming it, as well as to use and protect it. It was not in China or India where this scientific revolution was able to take off and flourish, but on the soil of Christianity. Cf. De Rosa, Guiseppe, *Cristianesimo, religioni e sette non cristiane a confronto* (Rome, 1994), pp. 141.

[185] Jean Guitton remarks: "Perhaps, I am most supported in my faith by the existence of saints." Guitton, Jean, *Che cosa credo* (Milan, 2003), p. 110. Raïssa Maritain and G. Consolmagno also regarded the existence of saints and the manifestation of sainthood in human history as one of the chief signs of the existence of God.

death, and he is most desperate because he feels that, owing to his sins, he could only "go to God empty-handed, with nothing done at all. It seems to him, at that moment, that it would have been quite easy to have been a saint. It would only have needed a little self-restraint and a little courage."[186]

In Esztergom, a provincial city in my country of Hungary, a family with six children was evicted from their home because they had not been able to pay their bills. It was only with great difficulty that they at last found a place to rent, a virtually unfurnished apartment. This family with six children, right before Christmas, was without furniture or food, not to mention gifts or a Christmas tree. One or two days before Christmas Day, a pickup truck pulled up in front of their apartment building. The driver got out and started carrying furniture, food, toys, a Christmas tree and decorations into the apartment. The mother watched this man, totally unknown to her, with astonishment. She asked him, "Where did you come from? And, first of all, who are you? How did you hear about us?" The man refused to say even his name. He got into his car and drove away. The woman could not believe her eyes. She just could not believe anything like this could happen. Thank God, things like this do happen. This, too, is one of the faces of Christianity.

The following story happened in Bissau Guinea, Africa. A child born in a little village in the jungle learned about a mission station in the nearby small town of Mansoa. He began attending catechism classes there. To go to the mission station, he had to cover the roughly six-mile distance on foot, and walk the same distance back home. The men in his village often gave him a beating for going to catechism classes, saying, "Why do you need the God of the white man? Why aren't you content with ours?" But no thrashing was powerful enough to make this kid give up his faith. Something had apparently captivated him. He would go again and again.

In the meantime, the boy grew up. He decided to have a genuine Christian family of his own. However, this was something that could not be done in his village, as the young people living there were not allowed to choose their spouses freely. He moved away, cleared an area for himself, and built a hut. Bissau Guinea was so simply organized that even the land was not parceled out. Anyone could build a house and cultivate a plot, wherever they liked. Then he abducted the girl he loved. The girl also became a Christian, and the two started their married life together. But the men in his village learned about his whereabouts. They came and destroyed his house, robbed him of his possessions, and severely beat him up, yet again. He sought refuge with the priests who had helped him so much in the past.

---

[186] Greene, Graham, *The Power and the Glory* (William Heinemann, London, 1940), p. 209.

In the few weeks that it took for the young man's wounds to heal, he came to understand that, in becoming a true Christian, he was not supposed to take revenge. He also understood that he had been set free, not to make only his life better, but to lift up others from his community as well. When he recuperated, he moved back to an area next to his village. He built a hut there and began to work in the field. As soon as the first crop was ripe, he put the bulk of it into bags and deposited them in the main square of his village as a gift, a present for those who had made his childhood a misery, destroyed his house, and thrashed him countless times. The people there could not believe their eyes. Next, he dug wells with the help of the priests. From that time, everyone in the whole neighborhood would go there to take water; they also got to see his family. The women eyed his one wife with envy (tribal communities there are still polygamous) and wished they themselves were loved as much as the two loved each other. They also envied their children because, in those tribal communities, the horrible custom of not letting male children grow up by their mothers' side continues to be the norm. The argument goes that a boy must be tough, and his mother would only pamper him. Thus, at the age of 3 or 4, they must be handed over to their aunts and uncles, causing great pain to mothers and children alike. The women looked at this man's family with envy because all of their children remained with them. Their children's faces, radiant with serenity and openness, also showed that they had been raised in a completely different environment.

When the teacher of the neighborhood died, nobody wanted to accept the job because the state did not give any payment for teaching. This young man, nevertheless, volunteered for the job. At the time of my visit (to help with well digging and other jobs, along with a group of young people from Italy), he was teaching 140 children on his own, in morning and afternoon sessions, in a "school" that was slightly larger than an average hut. In the evenings or at dawn, he would go out to the fields to do some hoeing to support his family. Then, one day, the roof of the school collapsed, but nobody cared. He nonetheless contributed whatever little money he had toward the repair, purchasing cement and felling trees so that the roof was eventually rebuilt. To him, those 140 children did matter. His eyes glittered as he was telling the story of his life. For him, the Gospel was not just a good narrative, it was his life.

XII. The Hope of Eternal Life

"Do not be deceived.
You will all die like animals,
there is nothing after death."

—German playwright and poet, Bertold Brecht

"If the dead are not raised,
'Let us eat and drink,
for tomorrow we die'."

—1 Corinthians 15:32

1. An ineradicable desire and intuition

The French writer Antoine de Saint-Exupéry reported that the Arabs tried to domesticate antelopes on the edge of the Sahara. They built enormous pens for them. But, when the desert winds began to blow, the antelopes started dashing about, and as if not seeing the pens, they crushed themselves to death. At that point, the Arabs experimented with rearing newborn antelopes in pens from the first day of their lives. However, when these grew up, and the winds picked up, they were also overcome by a strange kind of shiver and began to charge, fatally crushing themselves into the fences.[187] Antelopes were born to rush across endless savannahs.

By the same token, humans irrepressibly yearn for everlasting life, with intuitions about eternity in their hearts. Even prehistoric humans buried the favorite tools of their loved ones in their graves, in the belief that the deceased would need these. Egyptian pyramids are immense monuments to this kind of hope. The most important book of ancient Egyptian belief was the Book of the Dead, entirely focusing on the journey of the dead in the afterlife, as well as on the judgment and rewards awaiting them. Just as no religion-free human culture has yet been discovered, not a single human society is without manifestations of the hope of eternal life. Why is this world not enough for human beings? This was the question we attempted to answer in Chapter 3 (III/2) of this book. It appears that humans have intuitions or faint knowledge about what lies beyond this world.

2. The mystery of the human person

Humans may distance themselves from an object, but they can also connect with its reality. This is the basis of any human understanding. A physical or material entity cannot make this choice.[188]

The human person cannot be objectified. This may be likened to the relationship between the seeing eye and the field of view: the former will never be part of the latter. The reflection of an eye in a mirror is not capable of seeing. The subject involved in the process of cognition cannot be objectified, either.

Matter is governed by the human person. Someone deciding to raise their right arm at 12:43 p.m. may do so. The arm is not lifted because certain unique chemical reactions are initiated in the brain, which transmit a message to the muscles via the nerve tracts, instructing them to contract. What actually happens is exactly the opposite. At 12:43 p.m., intriguing chemical reactions start in the individual's brain because he or

[187]Saint-Exupéry, Antoine de, *Terre des hommes* (Paris, 1938), pp. 196-198.
[188] Cf. in more detail: Weissmahr Béla, *A szellem valósága* (Budapest, 2009), pp. 134-161.

she has decided to lift up his or her right arm.

Some argue that the human person is but an idea, that the self is a mere illusion, a projection of the working of the brain and of sensations. To those in favor of this theory (i.e., epiphenomenalism), we need to say that, were this the case, the truth of epiphenomenalism would also be zero, as it would also be only a projection of some chemical processes in the brain. In addition, we could also tell such a person that the whole of existence would be preposterous, if whatever we perceive as reality in the most basic sense (i.e., our very person) were not real.

But the human person is capable of understanding truth and reality (cf. III/7-8). He or she is perceptive of the moral commandments (III/6) and aware that he or does, indeed, exist. Reality has a very personal quality to it. Human beings can come to understand that nothing disappears without a trace. Energy is not destroyed but transformed. Why would it then be logical that the most important part of finite reality, the human person, should vanish into nothing?

From the final moment of earthly life emerges the human person, jettisoning the launch vehicle of the earthly body to acquire the reality of the spiritual body, as it is called in the Bible (1 Cor. 15:44), as the person enters a new life through the gateway of death.

151

3. The Resurrection of Christ

The Resurrection of Christ provided humankind with the ultimate assurance of hope in everlasting life.[189] The reality of this event has been described earlier, as well (VII/7).

A young person cannot be given hope by someone telling them, "Cheer up! You can do it! All will be well!" After all, human beings are not capable of drawing themselves up by their own hair. Only real hope, not generated by us, but surpassing us, can elevate humans and provide them a life worthy of a human being, created in God's image (cf. III/2.5).

The Resurrection of Christ has shown, once and for all, that God is real, and God is a living God Who can and will act. He has entered our world because we are infinitely important to Him.

If a person believes in life with God after death, they can be raised above themselves, above their limitations and selfishness. They can live with lofty ideals and hope, with a divinely informed conscience, with a sense of responsibility toward the common good, a magnanimous and generous heart, and with the peace that lies

---

[189] Other experiential evidence, e.g., the testimonies of people brought back to life from the state or proximity of clinical death, also seems to reinforce this assurance. Cf. Moody, Raymond, *Life after Life* (New York City, 1977).

beyond all human understanding (cf. Philippians 4:7).

4. The ultimate truth

Belief in eternal life also means that the moral order is headed towards ultimate fulfillment. This is why the imperfections of earthly justice can be tolerated. A Christian person can renounce vengeance and opt for non-violent means, because the ultimate Truth, in which everything will be rectified, does exist.

For many, the teaching of the Bible and of Christianity on eternal damnation presents serious problems. How could a loving God afflict and punish anyone for an eternity?

First and foremost, Christian teaching ascribes importance to the claim about the possibility of damnation because it is the ultimate guarantee of real human freedom. If damnation were not a realistic possibility, if there were only one predetermined way—life with God forever—then there would be no human freedom; everyone, in the end, would be forced to enter into God's eternal love. By contrast, Christian teaching posits that human freedom is so great that a human being can choose to say a final *no* to God and hence, to Love.

A Season in Hell
by Arthur Rimbaud

Once, if I remember rightly,
my life was a feast where all hearts opened,
and all wines flowed.
One evening I sat Beauty on my knees—
And I found her bitter—And I reviled her.
I armed myself against Justice. I fled.
O sorceresses, O misery, O hatred,
it was to you my treasure was entrusted!
I managed to erase all human hope from my mind.
I made the wild beast's silent leap to strangle every joy.
I summoned executioners to bite their gun-butts as I died.
I summoned plagues to stifle myself with sand and blood.
Misfortune was my god.
I stretched out in the mud.
I dried myself in the breezes of crime.
And I played some fine tricks on madness.
And spring brought me the dreadful laugh of the fool.
Now, just lately, finding myself
on the point of uttering the last croak,
I thought of seeking the key to the old feast,
where I might perhaps find my appetite again!
Charity is the key—
This inspiration proves I have been dreaming!
"You're a hyena still..."
the demon cries who crowned me
with such delightful poppies.
"Win death with all your appetites;
your egoism, all your deadly sins."
Ah, I've practiced too many!
—But, dear Satan, I beg you, an eye a little less inflamed!
And while awaiting my few cowardly little deeds,
for you who prize in a writer
the lack of descriptive or instructive skill,
for you, I tear off these few hideous pages
from my notebook of a damned soul.[190]

---

[190] (Une Saison en Enfer) by Arthur Rimbaud (1854 – 1891), translated by A. S. Kline

God never predestines or chooses hell for anyone. His desire is to see everyone in heaven with Him, where there is no more suffering, and there are no more tears. Heaven is our ultimate home (cf. Revelation 21:1-4). It is the human being who chooses hell of his or her own free will and does not contemplate leaving it, so filled with hatred for God does the soul become. It is we who disfigure ourselves, make the lives of our loved ones hell, and distort the world with our sins. It is not God Who condemns us to damnation, but we ourselves choose and create the state of perdition with our selfishness and opposition to the moral order set in place by God Who is Love.

Christian teaching is compatible with someone hoping and praying that no one will suffer damnation.[191]

5. God is good

If we look around at the world, we cannot but realize that it is amazing. This, in turn, could make us conclude that the One Who created it and from Whom our universe sprung must be Beauty, Goodness, Wisdom, and Life Itself.

We may not be able to imagine what will come after our death, and we do not actually need to imagine it. Through the gateway of death, we will arrive in the eternal Presence of God, and we simply cannot now comprehend the kind of life that will await us there.

It is sufficient to trust that the One Who created us in so much wisdom and Who presented us so richly with joy and beauty and love, did not do so just to make us taste happiness, then tell us afterwards, "You have had enough. The game is over!"

The world is not a strange waiting room, with every one of us waiting for our demise. Human life is not a macabre court case with the only verdict a death sentence for all defendants. No! The beauty of the world carries the promise of future fulfillment.

God loves humanity. indeed. We are infinitely important to Him. God has prepared a place for us in Himself. As Jesus said, "Do not let your hearts be troubled. You have faith in God; have faith also in me. In my Father's house there are many dwelling places... And if I go and prepare a place for you, I will come back again and take you to myself, so that where I am you also may be." (John 14:1-3)

[191] E.g., Saint Thérèse of Lisieux and Hans Urs von Balthasar. Cf. *Story of a Soul. The Autobiography of Saint Thérèse of Lisieux* (ed. M. Foley, Washington D.C., 2003) n. 52; Balthasar, Hans Urs Von, *Was dürfen wir hoffen?* (Einsiedeln, 1986); ID., *Kleiner Diskurs über die Hölle* (Ostfildern, 1987).

Gianna Beretta Molla[192]

Gianna Beretta Molla was a happy wife and a mother of three. When she met her older husband, Pietro, she noted in her diary: "God could not have presented me with a finer encounter. All I want is to make him happy." As a pediatrician, her contribution was remarkable, especially in relation to the children of the poor. She would regularly volunteer for various jobs in her local CRS (Catholic Relief Services) group, as well as at the parish office, and in conjunction with children's summer camps.

This undisturbed family life lasted until the fourth baby started "knocking at the family's door." Gianna's very first pregnancy checkup revealed that she had a large tumor on her uterus. As a doctor, she knew all too well what that meant. She was in urgent need of surgery. But she was also aware that it could cost the life of her baby. She told the doctor in the most resolute tone possible, "Save the child!" Her husband, standing beside her, did not even try to argue. He knew his wife. He wanted to be one with her in this final momentous decision.

The doctor performed the surgery without doing any harm to the baby. He walked out of the operating room with a face as white as a ghost. He said to the husband, "We have saved the child."

Then Gianna went home and arranged everything neatly, like someone going on a long journey. She returned to the hospital on Holy Monday, the day following Palm Sunday. Turning to a nurse, she said, "Sister, I am here. I have to die now." Her daughter was born just days later, on Holy Saturday morning. Gianna gave her the name Emmanuela, which means "God is with us." Two days later, she died.

I had the privilege to attend Gianna Molla's beatification ceremony in Rome. It was an indescribable experience. Her husband and children, including this youngest daughter of hers, who had since become a doctor, were also present. The daughter owed her life to the fact that she had a mother who gave life by laying down her own.

Blessed László Batthyány-Strattmann was a Hungarian physician, a doctor of the poor. When his son, Ödön, died at the young age of twenty, he went down the stairs to meet his praying family and said to them, "Now let us kneel down and thank God for giving Ödön to us for twenty years." Such was the faith of these people. It shone through even the darkest moments of their lives.

---

[192] Cf. Pelucchi, Giuliana, *Blessed Gianna Beretta Molla. A Woman's Life*, 1922-1962 (Pauline Books & Media, Boston, MA, 2002).

Wrinkles[193]

When I am old,
I would like to have wrinkles, a lot of them:
from laughs,
smiles, serenity, goodness,
and care for others.
I would like my whole life
to be on my face
so that everyone who reads it would say:
"This is a lovely story."

I desire my visage to be a countryside,
with hills and valleys,
where people lose and then find their way again.

Let its furrows be a hideout for joviality,
and may goodness and comfort
dwell in its corners.
Let there be plains
where people can rest
and ditches in which they may hide.
And I would want everyone to say,
"This landscape is breathtaking.

This is a human person."

---

[193] Anonymous author. Originally published in Hungarian in *Együtt az életért fenntartások nélkül* (Vienna, n.d.).

Dear Reader,

Goodness, Beauty, the Source of Life, your Creator, is knocking at your door. Perhaps, you are still uncertain about a few things or have some doubts. You do not need to be worried about that. If you believe that this world, with all the beauty and reason in it, was not created by itself, if you believe that people are important to God, and God has revealed Himself to us in Jesus, then you have the core of your faith and can, with all your heart, commend yourself to Christ.

Open the door to the One Who is knocking!

Wherever you are at the moment, your Creator is there with you. You were created by Him. When you were born, not only your parents rejoiced, but God did, too. From eternity, He willed that you would exist. He desires that you come to understand the mystery of love, for which He created you, and which He offers you. He died on the Cross for you, as well, taking your sins on Himself. After your death, He will welcome you with open arms at the gates of everlasting life.

Right now, at this moment, call out to Him:

Heavenly Father, I feel and know that You are knocking at the door of my life. Now I open the door to You. I believe in You. Please help my unbelief! I give thanks to You for the amazing world that You created, and for creating me. I give thanks to You for sending Your only Son into this world.

Lord Jesus Christ, I thank You for dying on the Cross for every human being, and for me. Forgive my sins. Now, I will let You enter my life. Now, I place my whole being in Your hands. Lead me in Your ways along the path of love.

Then try to find a Catholic church community where you will discover the Source of grace through the sacraments, and where you can receive further help as you travel through your greatest journey. May God's peace be with you!

BIOGRAPHY OF THE AUTHOR

BISHOP AND DOCTOR JÁNOS SZÉKELY

János Székely was born in into a large, deeply religious family in Budapest, Hungary. He completed his tertiary-level education in Esztergom, Budapest, and in Bethlehem, then continued his studies at the Pontifical Biblical Institute in Rome. He became a deacon in 1991 in Jerusalem, and later that year was ordained to the Catholic priesthood. Székely first began serving as a young priest in the village of Érsekvadkert, Hungary, where he was faced with both the extreme poverty and the rich values of the Roma gypsies in Hungary, who are pushed to the margins of society. Fr. Székely decided he would bring them the Good News, convinced that he could not simply sit in a parish and wait for them to enter.

"My gypsy brothers and sisters showered me with an enormous amount of love. There are few places where I have had the same good feeling that I had with them," Fr. Székely wrote about this period of his life, in the introduction to his book, *Getting Around the Gypsy World*. From this time forward, he continuously sought out more opportunities to transmit what he believes is the greatest treasure of all: Jesus' Good News.

Among other duties, titles, and accomplishments, Fr. János Székely served as a parish priest and seminary spiritual director, then as a teacher and rector for the Theological College of Esztergom. In 2007, he was appointed to be Episcopal Vicar for Social-Educational-Cultural Specialization and Titular Bishop of Febiana, as well as Auxiliary Bishop of the Archdiocese of Esztergom-Budapest. In 2010, Bishop Székely began serving as President of the Hungarian Council of Christians and Jews, and in 2011, he was the Church's chief spokesman in defense of the new Hungarian Constitution. In 2017, Pope Francis appointed János Székely as Bishop of the Diocese of Szombathely. With a portion of his heart still dwelling with the gypsies, he took on the leadership position of the Gypsy Pastoral Committee to the Hungarian Catholic Bishops' Conference.

Amidst all of his demanding duties and roles and titles, this list of which is incomplete, Bishop Székely continues to do his utmost to remain as accessible as possible to those he is called to serve. He believes it is vital for bishops to have a disposition of openness in order to be a human vehicle for God's care:

The shepherd should well know the life and problems of his herd. The shepherd has to take the lead, showing the way, then has to live inside the herd, listening to his people. Finally, he has to be present at the end of the herd to give a helping hand to the last ones, to the suffering.

Bishop János Székely firmly believes and witnesses with his life that we were all born to this world to learn how to love—to love everyone, but especially the sick, the elderly, the weak, and the poor.

In Bishop Székely's own words....

I was born in Budapest, Hungary, in the year 1964. My uncle fled from the country after the revolution of 1956, and thereafter lived in Germany. The memory of the Hungarian revolution against the communist regime was one of the most important factors that forged my identity. It was one of the most heroic events in the history of our nation, a courageous cry for freedom in a hopeless situation. My mom remembered it always as two weeks in Budapest in an ecstasy of joy. When the Soviet tanks appeared, however, many wept, seeing their entry as the annihilation of the best dreams of a nation. The painful absence of my uncle for many years was also an ever-present wound in our family, while at the same time, a reminder of his courage, which filled us with pride.

Our family was deeply faith-filled and patriotic. My father was a very talented engineer; my mother is a piano teacher. I have two brothers and one sister. Already at the age of seven, I felt the attraction, the vocation to give my whole life to God and to the service of others. One summer when I was fourteen, I read the entire Bible in three weeks while sitting under a tree: a decisive experience of my youth. When I was obliged to serve in the army of communist Hungary for a year and a half (as was every young Hungarian man in those years), I was jailed for five days in the small prison cell in the soldiers' barracks for possessing prohibited books—the Bible being one of them. For a half-year after that, I was not allowed to leave, trapped within the walls, called the *caserme*, that encircled us.

My studies were in Budapest, Bethlehem, and Rome. My doctoral thesis was about the Gospel of Luke, the structure and purpose of Luke's travel narrative. During my studies, I spent a summer in West Africa (in Guinea-Bissau)—an experience that transformed my vision of the world. There, my hands touched the extreme poverty of hundreds of millions and the cold selfishness with which rich western enterprises were exploiting the resources of that country, while at the same time, I experienced the flourishing of African Christianity.

Once I became a catholic priest, part of my work was with the Roma gypsies in Hungary—who comprise around 10 percent of the population—most of them poor, without education or jobs. The church runs community houses for the Roma children, where we help them with their studies, organize Bible study groups, and football teams. There, they can eat, wash their clothes, and dance.

I am responsible in the Hungarian Catholic Church for Jewish-Christian dialogue. We have edited a textbook about the history of the Jewish people in Hungary, one that is approved by Christian and Jewish historians and Church leaders, one that builds bridges in our society. Every year the church organizes a large collection in our catholic schools for Africa, and we have helped renew and rebuild an orphanage in the Congo.

During my service as Bishop of the Diocese of Szombathely, we have founded three catholic schools. These schools are a sign of hope in Hungary. Sometimes we save or rebuild the home of a very poor family, sometimes we provide shelter for the homeless, sometimes we welcome people fleeing from Africa, Asia, the Middle East... the Ukraine. I am grateful that I can be of help. I am happy that I can be a small light, a little sign.

NOTE TO THE READER

AMAZON REVIEWS:

If you were graced by this book, would you kindly post a short review of *The Door of Faith* on Amazon.com? Your support will make a difference in the lives of souls.

To leave a short review, go to Amazon.com and type in "The Door of Faith." Click on the book and scroll down the page. Next to customer reviews, click on "Write a customer review." Thank you, in advance, for your kindness.

OTHER BOOKS
BY QUEEN OF PEACE MEDIA

GO TO:

www.QueenofPeaceMedia.com/catholic-bookstore

VIDEO BOOK TRAILERS:

www.QueenofPeaceMedia.com/great-catholic-books

ALL OTHER ITEMS:

sacramentals, brochures, and more
www.QueenofPeaceMedia.com/shop

Available through
QueenofPeaceMedia.com and Amazon.com in
Print, Ebook, and Audiobook formats

THE MIRACULOUS MEDAL
PENDANT OF POWER

"The graces will be abundant for those who wear it with confidence."
**—Our Lady of the Miraculous Medal to
St. Catherine Labouré**

Learn why St. Maximilian Kolbe called It his Silver Bullet, why St. Mother Theresa called It her Medal of Charity, and why the world calls It Miraculous. Take a tour through the last two centuries of the most amazing collection of Miraculous Medal testimonies ever written. Discover how one small piece of metal has helped the sick recover, the blind see, the disbelieving come to faith, the desperate find hope, and even converted a High-Wizard satanist in a matter of minutes.

Free Miraculous Medals in bulk and Evangelization Packets, with cords sold at cost, are available now at **QueenofPeaceMedia.com**.

THE WARNING

TESTIMONIES AND PROPHECIES OF
THE ILLUMINATION OF CONSCIENCE
Revised and Expanded Second Edition

Endorsed by Msgr. Ralph J. Chieffo,
Fr. John Struzzo, Fr. Berdardin Mugabo, and more…

The Warning has been an Amazon #1 best-seller, ever since its release. In the book are authentic accounts of saints and mystics of the Church who have spoken of a day when we will all see our souls in the light of truth, and fascinating stories of those who have already experienced it for themselves.

"With His divine love, He will open the doors of hearts and illuminate all consciences. Every person will see himself in the burning fire of divine truth. It will be like a judgment in miniature."
—**Our Lady to Fr. Stefano Gobbi of the Marian Movement of Priests**

After the Warning brochures for mass distribution. Free to download and available in bulk at www.QueenofPeaceMedia.com.

WINNING THE BATTLE FOR YOUR SOUL

JESUS' TEACHINGS THROUGH MARINO RESTREPO, A ST. PAUL FOR OUR CENTURY

Endorsed by Archbishop-Emeritus, Ramón C. Argüelles
"This book is an authentic jewel of God!"
—**Internationally renowned author, María Vallejo-Nájera**

(See <u>The Warning: Testimonies and Prophecies of the Illumination of Conscience</u> to read Marino Restrepo's full testimony)

Marino Restrepo was a sinful man kidnapped for ransom by Colombian terrorists and dragged into the heart of the Amazon jungle. In the span of just one night, the Lord gave him an illumination of his conscience followed by an extraordinary infusion of divine knowledge. Today, Marino is hailed as one of the greatest evangelizers of our time.

In addition to giving talks around the world, Marino is the founder of the Church-approved apostolate, Pilgrims of Love.

This book contains some of the most extraordinary teachings that Jesus has given to the world through Marino Restrepo, teachings that will profoundly alter and inform the way you see your ancestry, your past, your purpose, and your future.

MANTLE CONSECRATION

A SPIRITUAL RETREAT FOR HEAVEN'S HELP

Endorsed by **Archbishop Salvatore Cordileone** and
Bishop Myron J. Cotta

(See **www.MarysMantleConsecration.com**
to see a video of amazing testimonies and to order)

"I am grateful to Christine Watkins for making this disarmingly simple practice, which first grew in the fertile soil of Mexican piety, available to the English-speaking world."

—**Archbishop Salvatore Cordileone**

CONSECRATION BOOK

"Now more than ever, we need a miracle. Christine Watkins leads us through a 46-day self-guided retreat that focuses on daily praying of the Rosary, a Little fasting, and meditating on various virtues and the seven gifts of the Holy

Spirit, leading to a transformation in our lives and in the people on the journey with us!"
—**Fr. Sean O. Sheridan, TOR**
Former President,
Franciscan University, Steubenville

ACCOMPANYING PRAYER JOURNAL

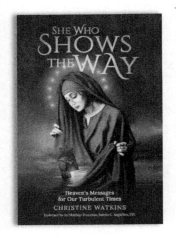

SHE WHO SHOWS THE WAY

HEAVEN'S MESSAGES FOR OUR TURBULENT TIMES

Endorsed by Ramón C. Argüelles, STL, Archbishop-Emeritus

"A great turning point in the fate of your nation…will soon be upon you…"

— **Mary's message of August 4, 1993**

TRANSFIGURED

PATRICIA SANDOVAL'S ESCAPE FROM DRUGS, HOMELESSNESS, AND THE BACK DOORS OF PLANNED PARENTHOOD

Endorsed by
Archbishop Salvatore Cordileone & Bishop Michael C. Barber, SJ

"Are you ready to read one of the most powerful conversion stories ever written? I couldn't put this book down!"

—**Fr. Donald Calloway, MIC**

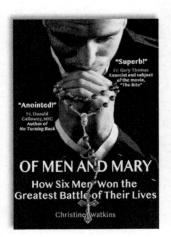

#1 AMAZON BEST-SELLER

OF MEN AND MARY

HOW SIX MEN WON THE GREATEST BATTLE OF THEIR LIVES

"ANOINTED!"—**Fr. Donald Calloway, MIC**

"Of Men and Mary is superb…miraculous, heroic, and truly inspiring."

—**Fr. Gary Thomas**
Exorcist and subject of the movie, "The Rite."

SERVANT OF GOD
FRANK DUFF

FOUNDER OF THE LEGION OF MARY

"This layman from Dublin, Ireland, multiplied a group of thirteen women into three million people—into the largest Catholic lay apostolate the world has ever known: The Legion of Mary. Discover the spiritual jewel of the story of Servant of God, Frank Duff."

FREE E-BOOK:
www.QueenofPeaceMedia.com/frank-duff

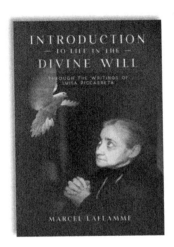

INTRODUCTION
TO THE DIVINE WILL

THROUGH THE WRITINGS
OF LUISA PICCARRETA

"Words will always be too poor to express what is experienced in the intimacy of the heart on discovering the "miracle of miracles": life in the Divine Will. The beauty of these truths charms the reader, and there is a captivating sense that the veil has finally been torn and heaven opened."
—Fr. Dominique Duten

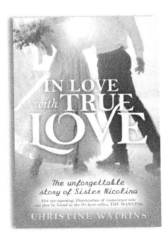

IN LOVE WITH
TRUE LOVE

THE UNFORGETTABLE
STORY OF
SISTER NICOLINA

This book is a privileged view into not only a charming soul and an enthralling love story, but into the secrets of Love itself.

To be notified of new and upcoming
Queen of Peace Media books,
sign up for our occasional newsletter:

www.QueenofPeaceMedia.com/newsletters

LIBROS EN ESPAÑOL

LIBROS EN ESPAÑOL

www.QueenofPeaceMedia.com/catholic-bookstore

EL AVISO
Testimonios y Profecías de la Iluminación de Conciencia

EL MANTO DE MARÍA
Una Consagración Mariana para Ayuda Celestial

EL MANTO DE MARÍA
Diario de Oración para la Consagración

TRANSFIGURADA
El Escape de las Drogas, de la Calle y de la Industria del Aborto, de Patricia Sandoval

HOMBRES JUNTO A MARÍA
Así Vencieron Seis Hombres la Más Ardua Batalla de Sus Vidas

PURPLE SCAPULAR

OF BLESSING AND PROTECTION
FOR THE END TIMES

**Jesus and Mary have given this scapular to the world
for our times!**

Go to **http://www.queenofpeacemedia.com/shop** to read about all of
the incredible promises given to those who wear it in faith.

Our Lady's words to the mystic, stigmatist, and victim soul, Marie-Julie Jahenny: "My children, all souls, all people who possesses this scapular will see their family protected. Their home will also be protected, **foremost from fires**. . . for a long time my Son and I have had the desire to make known this scapular of benediction…

This first apparition of this scapular will be a new protection for the times of the chastisements, of the calamities, and the famines. All those who are clothed (with it) shall pass under the storms, the tempests, and the darkness. They will have light as if it were plain day. Such is the power of this unknown scapular."

THE CROSS OF FORGIVENESS

FOR THE END TIMES

On July 20, 1882, Our Lord introduced THE CROSS OF FORGIVENESS to the world through the French mystic, Marie-Julie Jahenny. He indicated that He would like it made and worn by the faithful during the time of the chastisements. It is a cross signifying pardon, salvation, protection, and the calming of plagues.

FOR MEN AND FOR WOMEN:

Go to **www.queenofpeacemedia.com/shop** and click on "Cross of Forgiveness" to read about all of the graces and protection given to those who wear it in faith.

This bronze cross (1¾ inches tall and 1 inch wide—slightly bigger for the male) is a gift for our age and a future time when priests may not be readily available: "My little beloved friends, you will bear on yourselves My adorable cross that will preserve you from all sorts of evil, big or small, and later I shall bless them. . . My little children, all souls that suffer, and those sifted out by the blight, all those who will kiss it will have My forgiveness—all those who will touch it will have My forgiveness." The expiation will be long, but one day Heaven will be theirs, Heaven will be opened."

THE FLAME OF LOVE BOOK BUNDLE

THE SPIRITUAL DIARY OF ELIZABETH KINDELMANN

Go to www.QueenofPeaceMedia.com/shop to receive the Flame of Love book bundle at cost!

Extraordinary graces of literally blinding Satan, and reaching heaven quickly are attached to the spiritual practices and promises in this spiritual classic. On August 2, 1962, Our Lady said these remarkable words to mystic and victim soul, Elizabeth Kindelmann:

"Since the Word became Flesh, I have never given such a great movement as the Flame of Love that comes to you now. Until now, there has been nothing that so blinds Satan."

EXCLUSIVE HANDMADE BLINDS SATAN

THE MOST POWERFUL SCAPULAR YOU CAN WEAR

FLAME OF LOVE SCAPULAR

COMES WITH THE UNITY PRAYER THAT **BLINDS SATAN** AND A FREE BLESSED MIRACULOUS MEDAL ATTACHED

Go to www.QueenofPeaceMedia.com/shop to order the Flame of Love Scapular with the Unity Prayer that blinds Satan.